Paul Hostovsky

SELECTED POEMS

FUTURECYCLE PRESS

www.futurecycle.org

Published by FutureCycle Press
Lexington, Kentucky, USA

ISBN 978-1-938853-57-9

To Marlene

Contents

From
BENDING THE NOTES

From
DEAR TRUTH

From
A LITTLE IN LOVE A LOT

From
HURT INTO BEAUTY

From
NAMING NAMES

From
BENDING THE NOTES

(Main Street Rag, 2008)

Every American Child

will be issued a blues harmonica at birth
and taught to bend the notes because the notes
are for bending. And no American child
will lock his harmonica up in a harmonica case
but will keep it in his pocket all his life
so that any lost, scattered, fallen, foreign thing,
be it lint, pollen, tobacco, sleet or spiders,
may enter through the holes and take up
residence there. And every American child
will know how to inspect his blues harmonica
without assistance or prompts, unscrewing the tiny
bolts with his own fingernail, and without losing
them or the even tinier serrated square nuts,
remove the metal flanges and test each delicate
reed by plucking it with the same fingernail
to see if it rings true. And every American
child will be required to carry his blues harmonica
with him on his person at all times, and to produce
his blues harmonica when asked for identification
with the blues. And every American child will
be expected to learn by heart the history of the blues
because the history of the blues is an American
story, which some American grownups can't be trusted
to tell, much less sing, to their American children.

Coconut

Bear with me I
want to tell you
something about
happiness
it's hard to get at
but the thing is
I wasn't looking
I was looking
somewhere else
when my son found it
in the fruit section
and came running
holding it out
in his small hands
asking me what
it was and could we
keep it it only
cost 99 cents
hairy and brown
hard as a rock
and something swishing
around inside
and what on earth
and where on earth
and this was happiness
this little ball
of interest beating
inside his chest
this interestedness
beaming out
from his face pleading
happiness
and because I wasn't
happy I said
to put it back
because I didn't want it
because we didn't need it
and because he was happy

he started to cry
right there in aisle
five so when we
got it home we
put it in the middle
of the kitchen table
and sat on either
side of it and began
to consider how
to get inside of it

Bagpiper Among the Geese

I think it looks to them
like one of them,
this three-legged one
belly-up under
my arm, wrung neck
hanging down with my finger-
prints still on it.
I think they think
I've killed it,
till I squeeze with my elbow
and it comes to life
groaning, a three-
headed one now
craning its necks
over my shoulder, sounding
the alarm.
        The gander
lifts from his desultory nibbling
as if to consider
whether my domestic
squabble is impinging
on his honor, his distant
foreign and a little
ungainly cousin having eloped
with me, the interloper.
But is it love
or death, this alarming
embrace of mine,
all bellows and drones and tasseled
goose? He lifts
his bill skyward, tunes
his own broken clarinet a moment,
then resumes his nibbling,
returning his nose
to its own business
as if to say, Who knows
or cares if love is fighting
or love is loving?

And who dares
presume to understand love's ways
or love's eyes for the one
with the one leg and three heads,
or the three legs and no head?
And who's to say why one
is the one love is dying for
while another is a dead bore
at love's oblivious side?
There is only
this music that drones on and on
while someone or other is always
dancing till he drops
dead of exhaustion
or disillusion
or strangulation.
The indifferent
beaks will always go on eating.

Little League

When the ump produces
his little hand broom
and stops all play to stoop
and dust off home plate,
my daughter sitting beside me
looks up and gives me a smile that says
this is by far her favorite part of baseball.

And then when he skillfully
spits without getting any
on the catcher or the batter or himself,
she looks up again and smiles
even bigger.

But when someone hits a long foul ball
and everyone's eyes are on it
as it sails out of play...
the ump has dipped his hand
into his bottomless black pocket
and conjured up a shiny new white one
like a brand new coin
from behind the catcher's ear,
which he then gives to the catcher
who seems to contain his surprise
though behind his mask his eyes are surely
as wide with wonder as hers.

Deaf

That boy was good with animals.
And he was good *at* animals the way
some hearing boys are good at
making sounds of artillery fire
using only the tongues in their heads.
Using only his face and his hands
he could paint any animal on the farm
on the air, and we'd recognize it
by some detail he'd capture, some
unmistakable physical thing, an angle
or posture, a sideways chewing,
the dangle of a tongue, the puppy's ear hanging
inside out like a pocket.

He was the only witness when the neighbor's dog
got run over, and he told us the whole story
with his whole body, how the pickup
swerved to avoid her, grazing
her shoulder, the angle of impact
throwing her into the woods.
We all stood around, ignorant
of what happened exactly, hoping
and fearing as his story unfolded
and he embodied first the dog running, then
the truck braking, then
the dog then the truck then the dog
so we had the feeling we were seeing it all
just as it happened, and just as it was happening,
but in slow motion and with a zoom lens
and from six different camera angles.

Conversations with My Son

Houdiniesque and eight,
he snakes out of his seatbelt
on our way to Peabody Elementary,
and rests his little mug just behind my ear.
Here he puts a metaphysical question,
a prestidigitation of the mind:
"Where is Cleveland Ohio?"
And before I can answer, another:
"Would you rather be buried or
crucified?"
I ask if he means 'cremated'.
He asks me what's the difference.
I tell him and he says, "I just don't think
you should take up too much space
when you're dead, Dad."
For Pete's sake, I mutter.
And he's right there with another: "Who's Pete?
and what's Pete's ache?"
Together we watch the road to school
unfold like a familiar story
while I tell him the story of Pete,
the guy who said he loved Jesus so much
he would die for him.
That was his ache, I say.
But when the time came,
when the soldiers all came with their swords
blazing like the sun,
Pete got scared. And he ran away.
And he didn't do what he said he would do.
And that was Pete's ache, too.
"I think I'd rather be crucified," he says
as I pull in behind a school bus.
And I'm not quite sure if he means
he'd choose the pain of the nails
over the pain of the betrayal,
or the fire over a pine box in the earth.

Before I can ask him he's out,
he's unbuckled his belt, unlocked the door
and reappeared outside, running up the hill,
his little backpack full of tools
bouncing on his shoulders,
a head on his shoulders full of questions,
questions escaping all over.

Be Mine

I love mankind most
when no one's around.
On New Year's Day for instance,
when everything's closed
and I'm driving home on the highway alone
for hours in the narrating rain,
with no exact change,
the collector's booth glowing ahead
in the tumbling dark
like a little lit temple
with an angel inside and a radio
which as I open my window,
a little embarrassed by
my need for change
(until the silence says
it needs no explanation),
is suddenly playing a music more lovely
than any I've ever heard.
And the hand—
so open, so hopeful,
that I feel an urge to kiss it—
lowers the little life-boat of itself
and takes the moist and crumpled prayer
of my dollar bill from me.
Then the tap, tap,
tinkling spill of the roll of coins
broken against the register drawer,
and the hand returning two coins, and a voice
sweeter than the radio's music,
saying, "Have a good one, man."
I would answer that voice if I could—
which of course I can't—
that I've loved it ever since it was born
and probably longer than that.
Though "You too"
is all I can manage,
I say it with great emotion
in a voice that doesn't sound like me,
though it must be
mine.

Memory

My first best friend
was Charlie Lumly
when I was four
and he was four
I can still see his face
it was always dirty
or maybe it was only
freckled in which case
it was always freckled
in the house next door
where he lived until
he moved away
to another country
or maybe it was only
Pennsylvania
in which case it was a state
with a name like another country
and I never saw him again
though for a long time
I dreamed about him
because I think I loved him
or maybe it was only
a backyard kind of
dirty-kneed lust
that revives as soon
as someone else
named Clayton or
Cleveland moves
in next door

Trombone Lesson

The twenty minutes from half past nine
to ten of ten is actually slightly longer
than the twenty minutes from ten of ten
to ten past ten, which is half downhill
as anyone who's ever stared at the hillocky
face of a clock in the 5th grade will tell you.
My trombone lesson with Mr. Leister
was out the classroom door and down
the tessellating hallway to the band room
which was full of empty chairs and music stands
from ten past ten to ten-forty, which is half
an hour and was actually slightly shorter
than the twenty minutes that came before or after,
which as anyone who's ever played trombone
will tell you, had to do with the length of the slide
and the smell of the brass and also the mechanism
of the spit-valve and the way that Mr. Leister
accompanied me on his silver trumpet making
the music sound so elegantly and eminently
better than when I practiced it at home
for hours and hours which were all much shorter
than an hour actually, as anyone who's ever
practiced the art of deception with a musical
instrument will tell you, if he's honest and has any
inkling of the spluttering, sliding, flaring,
slippery nature of time, youth, and trombones.

Greenhouse

My Aunt Ellie lived in a green-
house. This was in Irvington
New Jersey. A Jew alone
is a Jew in danger, her husband
said. Their daughter, my cousin,
wanted to go where she wanted
to go. They said it was a big
mistake. In a greenhouse you
cultivate certain delicate
non-indigenous plants. The house
was green and my cousin fell
deeply in love with a black man.
When she married him her father
sat *shiva* for her, meaning that
he mourned her for dead. But
she was only living over in East
Orange. She had two beautiful
daughters who never knew
their grandfather on their mother's
side. Because she was dead to him
until the day he died. That was the day
we all went over to Aunt Ellie's house
where she was sitting *shiva.* We met
my cousin's husband Toe, for the first time,
and their two daughters, Leah and Aleesha.
And we opened all the windows in
the greenhouse on that day, for outside
it was a beautiful spring day and we
broke out the expensive delicate china
from Germany which they kept locked up
in a glass breakfront in the hall.

Dream

You're alive and riding your bicycle
to school and I am worried about you
riding your bicycle all the way to school
so I get in my car and drive like a maniac
through the dream over curbs and lawns
sideswiping statuary and birdbaths along
the way frantically seeking you everywhere
the rear wheel of your bicycle disappearing
around the next corner and the next and then
I am riding a bicycle too and sounding
the alarm which sounds like a bicycle bell
so no one believes it's an alarm and I pedal
faster and faster my knees bumping up against
the handlebars which by now have sprouted
ribbons with pompoms and a basket attached
with your lunch inside and I'm pedaling to save
my life and your life and finally when I find you
in the dream you aren't dead yet you're alive
and a little angry and embarrassed to see me
all out of breath on a girl's bicycle holding
your lunch out in my hand trembling with joy

Away Game at the School for the Deaf

Maybe we were thinking *ears*
instead of *hands*
and *eyes*. Stepping off the bus, we glimpsed
a flicker, then a flitting
from a sleeve. We felt
annoyed, then afraid,
like spotting an ant on the tablecloth, then
another and another till it hit us:
what we had on our hands was a nest,
a population:
everyone here signed
except for us, and our bus driver
was departing in our empty yellow school bus
leaving us standing there, wondering
where the gym was.

Once inside, we polished our lay-ups,
stole looks
at the deaf team polishing theirs:
we were taller,
but something in the air—tunneling, darting,
singing among them—
said *they* were quicker.
Their whoops when they scored, their groans
when the ball rolled round the rim full circle
and out,
were perfectly intelligible.
But the ref was at a loss:
he kept blowing his whistle but they kept on
dribbling to the hoop,
scoring points that didn't count.

Bicycles

It's like we're all bicycles
and we all have these handlebars
and some of the handlebars and some
of the seats are incredibly beautiful
not to mention the way the wheels spin
and the bells ring
and the reflectors reflect and we can't
look at them and we can't stop looking at them
and all we really want is to get on top of them
and ride off into the sunset but they say
hey I'm not a bicycle okay
I have an eternal soul that you can't see
because you're so focused on my handlebars
look they're only handlebars okay you're such a
foot all you think about is pedaling
all you think about is wind wind wind
so then we nod a little guiltily and maybe
finger a spoke a little sheepishly
and ask for their forgiveness
and maybe they feel sorry for us then
because our desire feels ugly to us then
when really it's beautiful
and they're beautiful and we're beautiful
and they lean over and offer us
their basket which is somehow attached
to the place where their handlebars meet and our lunch
is in there and their lunch is in there too
so we sit together munching our lunches
under the big trees
all desire gone for the time being
the wind playing up in the branches
our souls playing near our discarded shoes
kickstands gleaming in the late afternoon sunlight

Love Poem

I love this poem.
I would do anything
for this poem.
I am not above
stealing for example.
I stole in the past
and I stole from the past
and I'd gladly steal from your past
for this poem.
I would lie
for the sake of this poem.
I would lie in the face of this poem
just to make the poem face me.
Just to feel on my face the hot, sweet, faint
bad-tooth breath of the poem.
I could sink to anything.
I think I could kill.
I think I have killed
for the shape, the sheer
body of this poem.
Look how beautiful,
feel how impossible,
this slender, limned thing
weighing next to nothing,
saying next to nothing.
Saying everything.
Everything.

Not the End of the World

"Unhand her, vagabond," was my one line
in the school play. I had the part of the cop,
a minor role compared to Beth Levine's,
the heroine, or Billy Wiesenkopf's,
the vagabond. Still, I took my part seriously.
So although he forgot to *take* her hand, right on cue
I yelled, "Unhand her, vagabond," and it struck me
and everyone else, that my line made no sense. Then I knew:
this is the kind of mistake that will end the world.
A question of bad timing will hang in the air
like an empty trapeze swinging above the smoke
of that final disaster. Someone will utter a word
too late to take back, reach for a hand that's not there,
and "It's not the end of the world" will not be spoken.

Library Science

So my friend Craig is telling me how
he's going back to school for another
masters degree and this one's in library
science so I ask him how long it takes
to learn all there is to know
about shushing people and ciphering
library fines because I have a bachelors degree
in creative writing myself
which is yanking your own chain for your own
pleasure and if you're good for the pleasure
of others and if you're really good
they put you in a library where people
like Craig sit around all day shushing
the library wankers in whispers and tones
as benign as a library fine and that's
what I tell him now and what can he do
but listen politely and sip the cup of coffee
I bought for him because he's always broke
because he's always in school and owes
me at least that much as I expound
the science or art of wanking in a library
deep in the stacks without making a peep
without disturbing anyone and he can tell
from my description of the sensuous round mouth
and graceful slender index of the beautiful
librarian that I am speaking from experience
or else I have a gift for verisimilitude
as I indulge myself from my bookish point of view
behind the backbones of books I'm parting
on the sagging shelf where no one can see
me but I can see straight through to a librarian
I've created for myself and no other
a kind of contrivance a kind of seduction
approaching a kind of climax now which I refuse
to allow my friend Craig or any other
library scientist anywhere ever to thwart

Wincing at the Beautiful

So my friend Phil is telling me how
he can't get a date
how he loves women and how
they're always giving him looks
so I ask him what kind of looks
so he winces at the beautiful
braless young woman passing by
at that particular propitious moment
giving her a look of such
longing and longevity
that she returns his look with a look
that kills his entire family tree
from the roots to the unimagined
blossoms of the great grandchildren shriveling
on his shriveling bough
and I think I've diagnosed his problem now
and I think of quoting some lines from Rilke
but on second thought I think
a sports metaphor might serve him better
so I steer the conversation round to basketball
and the three second rule
which says you can only stand inside
the key for three seconds
before they blow the whistle
they're just blowing the whistle on you Phil
for breaking the three second rule
for standing there with your eyes
popping out like basketballs
it's a game like any other I tell him
then I ask him if he wants to score
and now that I have his attention
I throw in those lines from Rilke
I tell him that beauty is nothing
but the beginning of terror
we're still just able to bear
and the reason we adore it so
is that it serenely disdains to destroy us

and he winces again and this time
it's at the beauty of those lines
or maybe their truth which hits him
like a three-pointer now
that Rilke hits all the way from Germany
at a distance of a hundred years

Sighted Guide Technique

Ed Kochanowski is holding my elbow
and passing me the joint
between his thumb and braille finger
which is his reading finger, his index,
as we do-si-do two people wide,
high on our way to the Stop & Shop.
The Stop & Shop is his supermarket.
The weed is my weed. The fact that we
enter the store with a lit joint is an index
of just how high I am: I'm thinking
Ed is the perfect blind, no one will guess
it's the guy guiding the blind guy whence
the sweet familiar reek of cannabis
quickly filling the entire supermarket
as we tiptoe two people wide up aisle
one is emanating. "I thought I'd heard
all the dumb ideas about the blind,"
says Ed afterwards, digging the nail of his braille finger
into my elbow so hard that it hurts
as we shuffle home still high
under the crescent moon
banned for life from the Stop & Shop two
people wide. "So where's the roach?"
he asks me as an afterthought after
we've gone a block or two in stony silence.
And it's a funny thing about pain
but I start to laugh and he starts to laugh too
even though I haven't told him yet because
I'm laughing so hard that it hurts—
that the roach is under a pyramid of fruit
where I had the foresight, however late,
to ditch it just before they busted us
on the cusp of aisle two.

Breasts Poem

He went up to the poet after her reading
and told her he loved her breasts
poem. He paused after the word breasts
as though it came at the end of a line
in a poem about breasts. He was being
silly and also serious the way
breasts are silly and serious but she
didn't see it that way. She was
a very serious poet and she didn't
crack a smile. But her breasts poem
was full of the pleasures of connotations,
which he couldn't get out of his head—
jounce, for example, which sounds like
joust, which carries with it pictures
of women bouncing up and down on horseback
carrying poles under their armpits
called lances in the parlance of knights
at a tournament, the perfect word
for when a female passes by like
a song, like a poem with all the right words
in all the right places and he can't
get it out of his head, and he wants
to bash his head against another male head
just to get it out of his system because
whether he dies or whether he gets the girl
with the jouncing breasts, either way,
he will feel a hell of a lot better
than sitting around at a lousy poetry reading
in a flimsy folding chair, squirming
with desire for those lovely breasts rising
and falling, the lungs beneath them filling
with the poem as the poem fills his head.

Driving to Work with Britney Spears

I don't care what anyone says,
I've had to pee so bad in traffic
I've pulled over in the breakdown lane
where the courtships of small animals go on
in the ravines. I've been so full of shit
I've had to turn the radio on
just to drown me out. But I like
her voice. I like her signature
low note, that guttural thing she does
that sounds like pushing. Like she's
climbed down into a ravine and she's squatting
there among the animals, pushing.
It could be a bowel movement, it could be
a baby. It could be a second baby. Baby, baby,
it's very effective, whatever it is, and I don't
care what you think because I'm happy
singing along on my way to work,
my thumbs keeping time on my steering wheel,
my head full of bullshit and beauty and Britney
Spears pushing and singing and making babies.

Arse Poetica

Once in elementary school
I brought in my alimentary canal
for show and tell,

sat with it in the back row
of Mrs. Dysher's 3rd grade class, dying
for a turn,

stood up in front of the whole class
empty-handed,
nothing up my sleeve but a long

sleeve which I opened at one end
as wide as it would go,
panned my astonished classmates with the pink

circle of its entrance
ringed by a good number of deciduous teeth,
turned

and dropped my pants
and would have indicated the other
end with my index finger but

Mrs. Dysher jumped up and threw
her arms around me,
threw herself over me like a rug

and contained that little fire of an idea
without quite putting it out
(censorship as hug)

so that it blazes up on its own, again and again
still now,
consuming me, and I disappear.

Braille in Public Places

Touch me, I know you want to.
What would you say if I told you
I've never been touched in my life
by anyone who understood me?
And even if they were having
their convention here in this building,
squeezing into this elevator,
looking around for this restroom,
bumping gently up against each other like
a queue of balloons at this
ATM—do you think they would
see me, or even think to look?
I hate my life. I should have been
a poem by Li Po with a pond
and a frog, a soft rain and a pebble
the size of a braille dot thrown in.
At least I'd have something to do
with myself for eternity. I have
nothing to do with anyone. I am
someone holding up a sign
in an airport terminal, waiting
for a look of recognition to come
from among the arrivals who never
arrive. And it never comes. What
would that look even look like? Would I
recognize it? Is it round like
a smile? Is it pointed like a greeting
or a touch? Would I mistake it for
love? All of my life I have waited
to be touched by someone who could
touch me like that. I have given myself
goose bumps, look, just imagining it.

Failures of the Imagination

She was only attracted to blind men
but only congenitally blind men
whose idea of an attractive woman
was only an idea.

An attractive woman, you'd see her
guiding her latest beau down Main Street,
his head tilted upward and slightly to the side
like an erection at her elbow.

Of course there were misconceptions
especially among the eligible
sighted men of the town.
Some said her predilection

had something to do with braille
and bringing a woman to climax
by dotting her nipples.
Others said it was Oedipal

which sounded like edible
which led them all to imagine
masticating blind men trembling
on top of orgasmic women.

But there was one among them who
imagined what she saw in blind men
was what they saw when they imagined her.
He had a very good imagination

but still he couldn't imagine what that was.
He could only see that she was beautiful.
He could only close his eyes and still see it.

Getting Back at the Bullies of Junior High

You were nothing but question marks,
pushy, bellying question marks, weren't you? weren't you?
with no contexts but your chesty end-quote girlfriends,
turning up in my autobiography now, annoying

as typos. Why I oughta
delete you once and for all with one
stab of my little finger! And maybe I will!
But not before I'm done with you, not before

I've had some fun with you at your expense.
This is *my* turf now. My story. You could say
I'm God here, and you're...whatever I say you are.
And I say you are nothing but little bold face punc-

tuation marks, come to an unfortunate end, sentenced
to eternity in this poem which is kicking your butt
by making you the butt of every joke in it.
And I think it's going to be a very long poem.

And I think it's going to be published simultaneously
in many languages, and in all the best magazines
with the biggest readerships. And now I'm thinking
it will be the title poem of my next collection,

and also my Collected Works, to be published posthumously,
which I know is a big word for you, so let me tell you
what it means. It means I will be at peace, and you will be
still suffering eternal humiliation in this poem

which between you and me is beginning to bore me now. After all,
I have better things to do than waste my time
with your poem. Maybe I'll just throw it out with you in it.
Maybe I'll burn it. How about a little fire, question mark?

But it isn't over until *I* say it's over. And I say
it needs polishing. So go ahead, use your sleeve.
I'm going to sit over here now and take a nap.
It had better be brilliant when I wake up.

The Tush

Maraida Jenson's younger sister Inge
played Juliet in Mrs. Niedermeier's
school play. The part that got me in the
door to the Jenson house, and that much nearer

Maraida, whom I loved, of course, was Romeo.
Around this time my grandmother grew old
and died. I missed a week of school. The pretext, though,
of wanting to rehearse with Inge, failed

the way my dying-grandmother excuse
for playing hooky did—it too grew old.
And Inge saw right through it to my eyes
which couldn't look at Inge but behold

Maraida. Juliet. My grandmother's
strabismus always made her look half mad
or blind. I'd look in one eye then the other,
then settle on the middle of her forehead

and wonder, could she tell? It was a Jewish
funeral. *Yisgadal v'yisgadash*
sh'may rabbah. Somewhere there's a *tush*
in there. That always cracked me up. A *tush*

in a prayer for the dead. Maybe that was why
they put it in there. Lighten things up a bit.
It's like that play: He thinks she's dead. He dies.
She thinks he's dead. He is. She wasn't but

she is. It's so absurd, you have to laugh.
You have to learn to laugh again. So Inge
burst into tears before I'd gotten half-
way through it. Said she knew it all along.

I gave a great performance though. Maraida
never guessed a thing. Very convincing,
the Jensons called it. A picture even made the
local paper, of me dead, Inge wincing.

Visitation

I make him the best lunches though.
I mean I made his mother
a lousy
best friend.
I mean I made her a little
miserable.
So she kicks me
off the team
for being what she calls
a lousy team player.
I concede I am a lousy team player.
I never coached little league
or basketball
or soccer and I only
make it to a handful of his games.
But I make him the best lunches,
a sandwich to beat all sandwiches
every single Thursday
and every other Monday,
which he takes with him to school
in a brown paper sac
in a pouch on the abdomen of his backpack,
a sandwich to make his friends say
a little ruefully,
a little wistfully,
"Man, your mother makes the best lunches,"
when really it's his father
who engineers these miracles,
these visitations
of the angel of lunches,
these mothers-
of-all-lunches every
single Thursday and every
other Monday when I have him,
when he sleeps over and I have another
chance to make it
right.

Assembling the Bench Press

My son says this'll be a cinch.
He's 15 and says we follow the pictures.
I'm 46 and say we follow the words.
It has 87 parts and they all have names.
I find this reassuring as he hands me
a carriage bolt, an aircraft nut, a washer
as I lie on my back with an adjustable wrench
and pliers, and tell him the story of when I was
15 and walking home from school across
Taylor Park, minding my own business
when Nicky Vespa and Kenny Hovanek
and a redheaded girl whose name I think was Frankie
stopped me in the no-man's-land between
two baseball fields, for directions.
Nicky knocked my books down and directed
me to pick them up, then Kenny slapped me
hard in the face, then the girl looked
away. Then we all waited to see what
I would do. I got myself a bench press
from Sears and Roebuck. I was 15 and
motivated. Arnold Schwarzenegger was
undiscovered and bodybuilding in Austria.
My son quietly hands me the lat bar frame
and axle bushing. The only sound's the turn
of the screw, and me grunting underneath
the evolving machine. "But what did you
do? when he hit you?" he needs to know.
But in that moment, the moment
that got me started counting sets of reps,
thousands of reps in my basement night after night
gritting my teeth and trembling underneath
the oppressive weight of those two ghosts
and that red head still looking away—in that
moment that counted—I only fought back
the tears. Unsuccessfully. I line
up the pivot, secure it with a hex bolt, lie:
"It was 30 years ago, how should I
remember?"

From
DEAR TRUTH

(Main Street Rag, 2009)

Everyone Was Beautiful

The day that everyone was beautiful
was like any other day, the only difference
was that everyone was beautiful and the day itself
was a beautiful summer day or spring day or
one of those late winter days that smells like spring
and if it was fall it was early fall
when it's all but technically summer and everyone
was simply beautiful, not sexy beautiful
or movie star beautiful or drop dead gorgeous beautiful,
but everyone but *everyone* had this patina
of slightly bruised longing, this shimmer of
I think I knew you when we were children,
this look of I've loved you ever since you were born
and probably longer than that and it all started
with the paperboy careening out of the blue
dawn on his bicycle, pitching to the left and right
with his ballast of fifty today's papers
in a vast canvas sack slung over his shoulder,
balancing himself and the whole world
on the tip of morning, the streets beginning to stir
with shadows and workers and cars,
all of which were perfectly beautiful,
and it continued on like that throughout the day
with the gas station attendant and toll collectors
and motorists and pedestrians and clerks—
even the boss, even the boss's boss who always
seemed an ugly sort of fellow really, especially
on the inside. But on that day even the ugliness
was beautiful—it was a beautiful ugliness
the day that everyone was beautiful and the day itself
was a beautiful summer day.

Why It Hurts So Much

Because the pain was already in the body
the way the figure was already in the wood
before the knife revealed it

the body like a pile of splinters
growing around the glinting pain

the pain asserting itself like a birth
the body crumbling
falling away like a death

the pain was in the body
long before the body was in pain
long before the body was a body
the pain was there

and in the body before that body

the figure in the wood was in the tree
and in the tree before that tree

the pain is very old
much older than the body

which is why it hurts so much
and why the body cannot hold it

Why the Music Makes Us Cry

I thought it was just me until my Aunt Hannah
said no it wasn't just me it was just
everybody thinking it's just them until
the music saying it's everybody it's everybody
gets inside our heads and we nod our heads
in agreement with the music saying it's everybody
it's everybody it's everybody and we know it's so
we nod our heads to the music because we know it's so
and it's so sad to think we thought it wasn't
and it's so sad to think we will think that again
when the music ends we will think that again
and we shake our heads no at the thought of that
we shake our heads because the music is saying it's everybody
and that's when the tears start because we know it's so

The Perfection

On the way to bury you
a yellow BMW (a bee
among the mourners)

was weaving in and out of our little
lit line of grief
winding down route 22 to the cemetery.

It made me think of you—the restlessness,
the thoughtlessness—the way
he fell in line with us, then left us,

then the left lane slowed and he was back again.
I wondered if the sun drowned out the lights
that strung our private darkness faintly together.

Or maybe, seeing the lights,
he saw the darkness had the right of way
and swung into our midst to overtake us,

this acrobat among the yarmulkes,
now flying out in front, now closing ranks
behind the rabbi's car.

I always thought you'd recognize yourself
eventually, a long time afterwards maybe,
the way you used to be when you couldn't help it

or see it even, and seeing it finally,
and in someone else, it would feel a little like love,
only love a little too late.

Mostly it felt like perfection as we turned
that corner into the cemetery,
and out he shot, the bee, as from a jar,

as if he'd suffocate to death if death
contained him any longer,
a thin black cloud of exhaust

hanging in the air behind him, like a veil.

Sharing the Orange

First I hold it out to you
in my hands which are
trembling a little so you
take them in your hands
you take the orange in my
hands in your hands and you
stop my trembling first
then you kiss me with your
eyes wide open and I feel your
hands on the orange and I
hear the skin tear open
I hear your fingernail tear it
ripping it back without taking
your eyes away from my eyes
all this you do without looking
you guide my finger to the wound
and you press my finger into it
and together we peel the rest of it
completely away without looking
away from each other's eyes the wet
soft creature of the orange sitting
naked in our hands the smell of it
rising like a sunrise on our fingers
which we hold up to our noses
and put into each other's mouths
sharing the orange without eating it
tasting the orange without eating it
without looking and without looking away

That Light

Everything is interesting
if you're of a mind to see it
in that light. Claude Monet
probably understood this. The stoners
back in high school definitely
understood that everything is intoxicatingly
interesting if you're of a mind
to see it in that light. My grandmother
in the emergency room
surrounded by doctors and nurses and children
and grandchildren, was of a mind to see
the pulse-oximeter on her left index finger
as the most interesting thing in the room,
more interesting than anything else in recent
memory, which was mostly gone
by then anyway. She cocked
her head like a bird or philosopher
contemplating a crumb
on God's table under the light, that light,
and said to her children and her children's children
and all of the strangers working together
to keep her from dying: "What
is the name of this thing? It's so interesting.
I don't think I've ever seen it before."

Dear Truth

I do not love you.
I am running away
with my beloved
illusions. The sweet
nothings. Nothing
is what it seems.
I love what seems.
I am crazy in love with
the painfully obvious
transparent surface.
I am simply hungry.
You keep the house
and everything in it.
I am taking the dog.
And the windows.

Eulogy

We were all a little in love with him. He was
a little in love with himself. That sublime
self-centeredness of the true artist. Which didn't
change the fact that he was a selfish prick
and a compulsive masturbator in the figurative
and probably the literal sense. But he was beautiful.
So you couldn't blame him for it. And you couldn't
look at him and you couldn't stop looking at him,
as though beauty were a kind of deformity—
you looked then looked away, then looked some more.
As though your eye were the fly, beauty the open
sore. It was like an affliction. His affliction, and yours.
Yours because it hurt, he was that beautiful. His
because as it faded, I think he finally began to live.

To a Motion-Activated Paper Towel Dispenser

Once upon a time we touched things.
We touched each other, we touched
ourselves. The world had
doorknobs. You could grab ahold of the world
and walk right through it. There were
handles, beautiful handles, and we
couldn't stop pulling them.
Hand washing hadn't caught on yet
so people caught colds from each other and worse,
much worse. Most people couldn't
even spell prophylaxis, much less
practice it. But there was such a thing as
olfactory intelligence. People loved smells
more than books. An armpit
was a library or a temple. You could
worship and study there. And you could
sniff your own fingers to get
word from your lover
more eloquent than a hundred love letters.
But today it's no longer possible
to just open a window and make love to the world.
Today you can't even
touch yourself and feel good about it anymore.
And the children's drawings
are full of emaciated stick figures
with lumpy limp smiles
and stumpy arms whose hands can't reach
below the equator.

Visualization

Your pain is a television
mounted on the wall
at the Dunkin' Donuts
where you sip your coffee
and look out the window
at the trees. It's difficult
to ignore the peripheral flickering
distracting you from the poem you want to write
about the trees. You have tried
changing your position. You have tried
changing your mind
about the television,
simply allowing it, giving in to it,
giving the television your full attention,
being with the television.
But the only thing that's on is
so bad it's sickening. So you just
keep on looking out the window at the trees.
It's winter or late fall and this one
sickly-looking tree across the street
has snagged the red kite
of your attention. It's almost completely bare
except for a little red, and it looks like
a cancer patient in a johnny with
its butt hanging out and a red
kite or mortification in the crown.
And it seems the poem is beginning to take shape
in your head in spite of
or because of the television. Because just yesterday
in radiation oncology where
there are no televisions so everyone
is usually reading or talking or sitting
quietly alone with their thoughts, there was this one
sickly-looking guy coming out of the changing room—
and he looked like this tree with the red kite in it,

because his skin was kind of gray,
and tight, and peeling, and his arms were
lifted up above his head, his hands trying
to tie the elusive string of his johnny
which was like the string of a runaway kite,
and his butt was hanging out, and his television
was laughing at him, and your television was
silent. Blank. There was something wrong with your television.

Hypochondriacal

I thought I was dying but it was nothing.
It seems to be happening more and more often.
It's the kind of nothing that's something

the way a coat hanger swinging
in an empty room you keep coming back to
because you think something is in there, is nothing—

the way a current of air,
or a rise in the wind, or an almost imperceptible
drop in the temperature, is something.

Some things are more themselves than others.
Some are lymphomas and some are lipomas,
and sometimes all the worrying's for nothing—

the fasting, the testing, the blood-work and x-rays,
the invasive, exploratory, tortuous, torturous
procedures turn up nothing. Something

poetic about a lifetime of saying
you're dying. Something hyperbolic.
Something metaphoric. Nothing
like a good metaphor for saying what something's like.

Sick Well

He was good at being sick.
After all, he'd been sick for
a very long time.

It wasn't a salable skill
at first. But when more and more people
began to get sick

he realized he knew something
they didn't. When you're sick
be sick. That

is how to be sick well.
How to be sick well would eventually
become the title

of his first book, which was a best seller.
People who got sick read it
and learned how.

And it was a revolutionary book because
throughout history people who got sick
tried to get well

and often died trying. But no one
had ever thought of trying
to be sick well. That

was truly something new. And dying well
would have been the title of his second book
but he died well

before it could.

The Nurse's Office

I like it here. I don't feel sick
but I don't feel good exactly either.
I like it when you ask me questions
about how I feel and since when.
I don't know how to answer them
exactly. It hurts here, and here. It feels
good to be touched and puzzled over.
I think if anyone can solve the puzzle
you can. I like your stethoscope
on my skin. And your eyebrows
coming together over my underlying
condition. I like your new thermometer
in my ear, but I liked the old one better
under my tongue, with its promise
of you returning in 3 minutes to read it.
Now I sit here in this chair with my
symptoms while you write at your desk
all the way over there. Out in the hall
it's quiet. The only sound's the sweep
of the long broom—Tony our custodian
pushing his way up the infinitely tessellating
checkered floor with his jutting elbows and rose
tattoo climbing. The coast is clear. See you
tomorrow, I say, and slip back out
into infinity before you look up.

Word Problem

If a man in St. Paul, Minnesota
is writing a poem on a bus
going 25 mph,
while across the street a woman
sets her alarm for 6:15 and begins
undressing, how long
before a dreamy back-row kid in algebra
figures out he's fallen tragically in love
with the words,
which in algebra are in the employ
of the numbers,
which is the problem,
and the tragedy,
and the poem,
which says the words are like liveried servants
standing around the bleak table
of the numbers
without any underwear on,
attentive, attractive, redolent
of the pleasures of connotations,
but keeping a respectful distance
which is approximately equal to the distance
of the boy from the woman undressing,
plus 10 or 20 years,
minus the population of St. Paul,
in a room with only a bed in the middle
with a sagging mattress,
like an equal-to sign with a squiggly mark—
an approximately-equal-to sign—
where she stands on one side
forever undressing,
and he sits on the other
daydreaming
in the back row
of infinity?

A Woman Taking Off Her Shirt

does so with arms crossed
over her belly
like she's hugging herself
and each hand takes hold
above the opposite hip
and off it comes in a fluid
motion like a fountain shooting up
and falling down in a great arc
the shirt rising up and the breasts
rising and falling and the hair
falling and finally the hands
falling to her sides with the shirt
in one hand inside-out

while the man
taking off his shirt
wrestles it off
grabs his own collar first
like he's going to beat himself up
then dips his chin down like a fighter
into the dark well of the shirt
and climbs down in it
reaching back and grabbing ahold
and pulling it up over himself
and pulleying himself
down through it and out.

The Sadness of Dads

It was there in the eyes of the silverback
in the nature documentary on gorillas,
sitting apart from the rest of the group,
chewing, looking past the females
and the young he had sired, up toward
the mountaintop, which was partly obscured
by mist. And it was there underneath
the bellying way he swaggered up
to one of the smaller males, did a chest-beat,
gave a threatening growl and bared
his teeth. And there it was again inside
the waiting, when the whole group looked
to him to make the first move, to lead them
up the mountainside in search of another
bamboo patch. And finally, unmistakably,
it was everywhere, smeared all over the grass
and in the air all around, in the sickening silence
and the unrestrained weeping of one of the four
research biologists walking beneath the poles
which bore the mutilated body, the prized hands
and head cut off by poachers with machetes
and wives and children of their own.

On Adversity

I'm wishing now I'd read that book on adversity,
the one the blind mountain climber wrote
about climbing mountains and not looking back,
but looking straight ahead, or inward, or maybe
upward—I forget now where he said to look
in the face of adversity, because I only read the review
and the excerpt, and I don't think that was enough
to see me through. Which is why I'm wishing now
I'd read that book on adversity when I had
the chance, now that I have no chance, no net, barely
a toehold, and the ropes have gotten twisted
round my neck. I could use that book right
about now. And yet I wonder, even if I'd read
that book, would I have the wherewithal to look
where it said to look? Would I remember to do
what it said to do, to clinch salvation in a pinch? I think
not. I think there is no way to prepare for this. This is not
a test. Though some will pass with flying colors.
And for others falling will be a kind of flying.

Man Running for Bus in Harvard Square

This is a poem about seeing it both ways,
about an idealist running for a bus and a
realist driving that bus and seeing a hopeful
expectant runner waving high and meaningfully
with his briefcase flopping against his thigh
and his excellent tie flapping in his face
as he sprints toward the slowly departing bus,
the bus which is departing, which is to say
moving away from the curb, so you see it isn't
stopped. If it were stopped it would be another
poem altogether, but this poem is about a man
who believes in communication and is running
and waving a hand at a moving bus and another
man who believes this man has missed this bus
and is driving this bus and sees this man trying
to stop a bus with a wave of his hand and a
briefcase full of papers—briefs or notes for a
class at Harvard perhaps—and he chooses not
to stop the bus but rather to drive right past
this idealist from Harvard who has missed the bus
and thinks he can reverse it or revise this with his
hand, as though it were words, as though it weren't
what actually happens, but he can't, no, not this.

Shopping for Beds on a Snowy Evening

We take off our boots
to try on the bed
at Sears. It's a little too
public with those teenagers
climbing the Stair Masters over there,
that large family arguing
in Spanish among the refrigerators,
this sales clerk in his pimples
hovering above our headboard,
spouting dimensions, promotions, double
entendres. We lie here in
traffic, love and a frank
mischief in your eyes. "We'll
take it," you tell him and clamp
your mouth on my mouth,
and we start to roll around
as a hundred humming appliances
praise the king-
size bed as big as a boat
you just bought for us
for a thousand dollars, the sales clerk
swimming tactfully away on his clipboard
to ring us up.

The Long Poem

Tall men in wheelchairs grow
famous, for having been tall—they're still
tall, of course, but now they're more like
people who were famous once
and no one remembers their fame, so they grow
smaller somehow. Sometimes you can tell
from their big hands or feet or orotund
voices that they were tall—that they *are* tall—
but it's hard to remember because they're always
sitting down now. No more standing ovations
for people who were famous once, I was thinking
on the fourth floor of Aspinwall, waiting
for Mr. Rodewald to come. He was late for class.
The class was called The Long Poem. It was the end
of the semester. We'd already read *The Iliad*,
Byron's *Don Juan*, Wordsworth's *Prelude*,
and Tennyson's *In Memoriam*. We were reading
The Loom by Robert Kelly now. Kelly
was Rodewald's friend and colleague. Kelly
was prolific and prodigious—6'4",
400 pounds, with a beard that reached his testicles,
and twenty poetry collections under his belt
already by the time I was 18, a freshman
at Bard, and a little in love with Mr. Rodewald.
Great writers grow famous, but great readers
just keep reading quietly to themselves,
and sometimes aloud to others. Rodewald
was a great reader. And he liked to read to us
aloud at the beginning of class. First we'd hear
the elevator *ding* out in the hallway, then
he'd kick the door open with the battering ram
of his leg-rests, and park the wheelchair up front
at the long table, and put on the brakes, and remove
first one leather glove and then the other. Then
he'd sort of ruffle his long legs by lifting them
by the pant-legs, giving them a shake, and setting them down
the way birds will half-open their wings, then settle them
back in, tucking them in to get comfortable.
Then he'd take out his briefcase and open it

in his lap. And take out the book and open it
to the page—all this without saying a word
to us—not hi; hello; good morning; Laura, you're
looking beautiful as ever—nothing. Then, finally,
he would begin to read. To us. And he'd go
a solid thirty or forty minutes, not saying
a word of his own, saying only the poem,
the poem that he'd been reading for longer
than we'd been living, relishing it like a meal
in front of us, like a man eating a great meal
all alone at a long table. I remember once
in the middle of Homer, someone drifted off
and started snoring softly, tricklingly...
Mr. Rodewald stopped reading, closed the book,
lifted it high above his head like a spear, took
aim—and sailed it across the room with bellying
pages, nailing the poor sleeper on the temple
and cheek, which blanched, and reddened, and trickled
a little blood. The stricken student sank
deep in his chair, terror in his eyes, then disappeared
out the door forever. Routed! *Sing, Goddess,
the anger of Peleus's son...* Mr. Rodewald
was heroic. It was partly his short temper, partly
his short black beard, and partly his biceps
which were thigh-thick from pushing
and pulling his own weight up and down our hillocky
campus. Always in my dreams he was standing,
walking. But in class he was Achilles, seated
in his chariot after great battle, or resting
in his tent after much fornicating. I suspected
he was fucking Laura Callahan, that beautiful
diffident sophomore whom I'd seen
getting into his car, a Buick Skylark fitted
with hand controls for the brake and accelerator.
I imagined a tall man in a wheelchair
making love to a beautiful young woman
slowly, tenderly, intelligently. I imagined
the two of them using the wheelchair as a prop
in their lovemaking, the way two hungry lovers
in a kitchen might enlist a chair or table
or countertop, before ending up in the bedroom or

on the kitchen floor... But where was Rodewald now?
We'd been waiting on the fourth floor of Aspinwall
for twenty minutes. No elevator *ding.* No leg-rests
crashing through the door like the Achaians
in their strong greaves. I stepped out into the hallway,
took the elevator down to the ground floor,
and started down the path that led to the handicapped
parking area, though first it meandered between
the bookstore and theatre, past Buildings&Grounds
and Robert Kelly's office with its big
bay window. And there was Rodewald, stuck
behind a red B&G truck parked
across his path. Someone had backed it up
to the loading dock of the theatre, where it stuck
way out. And he couldn't pass. He was sitting there
reading. There was no one around—
no driver, no B&G guys, no students.
Just me and Rodewald and the truck
and the book. He looked up vaguely, asked me
if I knew how to drive a truck. I said sure
thing. Then I climbed up into the cab, and lo,
the key was in the ignition. There was a long
black stick-shift with a ball handle, and three
pedals on the floor. I remember wondering
what the third one was for. I looked out the window
at Rodewald smiling conspiratorially. I released
the emergency brake and the truck started to roll.
I put my foot on the clutch, which I assumed
was the brake. I was an English major on a roll. Kelly
was breathless from climbing his long poem. Rodewald
was hiking the book between his legs and going out
for the long one, the bomb. The crowd went wild
as the truck crashed into the wall and my head
hit the windshield—touchdown! Miraculously
I was unhurt, the truck was out of the way, and Rodewald
was laughing. He was laughing so hard that I thought
he might tip over. I wanted to laugh with him but
I couldn't stop shaking from the shock. And then
we were walking together, as in a dream,
back to The Long Poem, leaving the scene
of the accident for others who came after to interpret.

From
A LITTLE IN LOVE A LOT

(Main Street Rag, 2011)

Little Things

Me and Beth Jeannette had a little thing.
This was a long time ago when my
thing was little and I didn't know anything
about such things. Somehow we ended up
upstairs in her bedroom on her bed
with her face very close to mine and a little
pimply. Her eyes were soft, her hands were
busy. My hands were folded politely
in my lap, as though waiting for tea or
poetry. My eyes, roaming the walls, found
an M. C. Escher print with tessellating
staircases and climbed them peripherally
while Beth continued to block my view
with her nose. In the end, our little thing
was like those staircases—it went nowhere
though it seemed to be going somewhere,
especially when she touched my thing and I
had to go to the bathroom. All these years later
I look back on that little thing with fondness,
tenderness, and a little sadness, as though
I were looking back from deep within infinity
at my first tender, tentative tessellations.

Exegesis

We couldn't have been more than twelve
or thirteen, sitting on that green bench in the late
sixties or early seventies, me and Michael Zucker
who was much more savvy and world-weary
than I, when I asked him to please explain
the meaning of the words to a song by Carly
Simon, who was simply gorgeous—that much was
plain—after we'd resolved the essential question
of whether or not she was wearing a bra
in that photo of her with the blue top and thick
lips on her album cover. "I don't get it," I said.
"'You're so vain. You probably think this song is about you.'
But the song IS about him, isn't it?" I asked Zucker,
holding my palm up in the air like one who is
trying to ascertain the truth about whether or not
it has started to rain. Zucker looked away then,
gingerly fingering the green slats, as though he were
reading the carved names of the lovers and obscenities
tactually. Then he took a deep breath and exhaled
miserably, took the album cover out of my hands
and gazed awhile at Carly Simon who was gorgeous,
famous, braless, and older than me and Zucker put together.
"That's the point," he said. "She's in love with him."

The Debate at Duffy's

She said that sex was a yearning of the soul.
He said it was a very compelling argument
of the body, a compulsion. She said it was
a spiritual compulsion. He said it was nothing
if not carnal, *carni,* meat. This conversation
took place in a bar. The background music was
so loud it was in the foreground. The bodies
on the dance floor were moving in ways that
would interest even the dead if they could only
remember how to live. There was a baseball game
playing on television. On the table were two
empty glasses, and the bottle's green phallus
which she took in her hand and pulled toward her,
pulling him toward her as she poured them both
another drink. He drank deeply, felt the spirit
filling his cup. Then he looked into her eyes and saw
that she was beautiful, sexy, and—at the bottom
of the 9th—suddenly, surprisingly, irrevocably, right.

The Affair in the Office

It belonged to all of us in a way
because we all shared
in the surprise
that it existed at all,
and also, privately, in the thrill
of the two lovers
(none more surprised than they)
who'd worked together in the same sad office
with all of us for all
these years, and both of them married,
and both unhappily. It was
a sad office, like so many
sad offices, full of the inexorable sadness
of cubicles, and computers, and empty
of love. Or so we thought. For no one
saw it growing—it must have
gotten in through a high
bit of laughter in the lunchroom,
then a glancing away
and a looking back again, the way
it sometimes does. And when it got out
in whispers around the water cooler
we all drank from it,
we drank it in, and in this way
it refreshed us, and amazed us,
and belonged to us because
we all took it home, took it
with us in the car, or on the train, sat with it
in rush hour, shaking our heads as though
we were listening to music, and in a way
we were listening to music,
shaking our heads and smiling,
looking out the window, fingers drumming.

Battling the Wind and Everything Else

My neighbor—the one with the flagpole
and the flag, and the pickup truck
and the patriotic bumper sticker, and the perfect
lawn and the leaf-blower with the power pack—
never seems to see me when I wave to him.
In fact, I am trying to get his attention
right now, but his eyes are on the enemy,
the leaves. He is aiming the long barrel
of his leaf-blower at them and blowing
them away. But the wind is counting its money
and throwing it away all over his lawn.
He is Sisyphus pushing one red leaf or another
up the berm of a perfect lawn forever. And I feel
sorry for him, the way I might feel sorry for
a large carnivorous bird in a shrinking ecosystem
on the nature channel. I know when he looks at me
he sees a guy who is half-heartedly, half-assedly
raking the leaves around on a disgrace-of-a-lawn
the way a kid pushes the peas around on his dinner plate
with his fork, trying to make it look like there are fewer
peas than before, when really there are still the exact
same number of peas; and he sees the leaves messing up
his lawn as *my* leaves, because *his* leaves are all in order—
he sees to that. So the ones that are crossing the border
and have no right to be here, and should just go back
to where they came from, must be *mine.* I see this all
written on his face as he grits his teeth and stares
the dancing leaves down, then blows them up
over the edge of his property. But they keep on
dancing back again because there's a party
going on here, and the wind is counting its money
and throwing it away. So I walk right up to him—
I get right in his face so he can't not see me,
and I wave hello. He disengages his leaf-blower,
after revving it a few times first at the intersection
of our meeting. And I say to him, "I've been trying
to get your attention." And he says, "You got it."
And I say, "How you doing?" And he says, "Battling
the wind and everything else." And I say, "I can see that."
And he says, "How *you* doing?" And I say, "Good. Good."

If Not for Stephen Dunn

This poem is not for Stephen Dunn.
It's for the one whose Stephen Dunn I stole
out of a hospital waiting room
when no one was looking,

when he or she—when *you*
(I like to imagine you're a she)
got up to go to the toilet maybe,
and sat there thinking
(I like to imagine you sitting on a toilet, thinking)

about a poem by Stephen Dunn
lying open and face-down
out on the waiting-room table where you left it,
a little naively perhaps,

among the magazines—
an expensive cut of meat on a bed of jelly beans,
cooling on the sill of the world

where I found it
when I entered feeling ravenous
and symptomatic,
thinking

you only live once,
and feeling
justified in stealing this book,
stuffing it into my yellow backpack like enough
food for one person for one year.

A year later I returned it.
It was one week after 9/11. Policemen
were stationed in the hospital corridors then.

I must have looked guilty, shady, unshaven,
like a terrorist trying to plant
fifty stolen poems by Stephen Dunn
on a waiting room table full of magazines,

for they stopped me
just inside the doorway,
and asked me politely and dead
seriously

to remove my yellow backpack.
Two secretaries, a nurse, several patients
(I like to imagine a liver recipient
sitting somewhere among them) looked on

as two thick and inarticulate
constabulary hands,
trembling, drew out
and held up under a light, under a nose,

this bundle of devices
with enough combined force to take
at least 3 lives—
yours, mine and Dunn's—
completely by surprise.

German

I thought it sounded strong, impressive, Germanic,
to say: "I have to go to German now." I imagined
my friends all staring admiringly at my back
as I walked industriously down the tessellating hallway
to German, my posture slightly straighter, my rucksack
slightly heavier with Dieter and Petra inside dialoging
about Bratwurst and Goethe and Turkish guest workers.
I could recite "Der Erlkoenig" by heart, and my r's
were perfect drum solos. Nancy Baum sat in the seat in front of me
and pretended not to hear when I whispered: *Ich liebe dich*
into her umlaut—that pair of moles on her left earlobe.
I thought it sounded romantic, Germanic, productive
as a cough. Frau Spier thought so too, for she asked me
to repeat it for the benefit of the whole class. Nancy's
earlobes blushed then, and her umlaut looked
like two watermelon seeds. Later that semester
I translated one of Rilke's sonnets to Orpheus,
the one about the tree and the ear. My translation
employed an umlaut where no previous translator
had ever thought to. I thought it was brilliant, subtle,
Orphic. I published it in our high school lit mag
and waited. I waited twenty years. Then, suddenly,
there she was in front of me again, with her back to me
at the reunion, lifting a mixed drink to her lips with a slender
ringless hand at the bar, the umlaut right where I'd left it.
I whispered: *Ich liebe dich,* and she turned around, the wall
finally down, smiling a smile as wide as East and West.

50-Year-Old Circuitry

He looks at all the beautiful women
especially all the young beautiful women
especially all the old-enough-to-be-her-father
beautiful women and he feels a little
ashamed of himself
but he also feels that what he feels
is a sign
that he's alive
in fact it's the only he's alive sign that's still
got all the bulbs burning
brightly inside of it
so whenever he sees a beautiful young woman
like his daughter's friend Courtney for example
whose body is a precocious
light bulb and whose face is a pure
light
he can't look at her and he can't stop looking at her
and his eyes turn into neon I'm alive signs
alternating with the all-night
SEX signs flashing in the red light district
behind his vanishing hairline
so the combined effect is a kind of
I'm STILL fucking ALIVE sign
which lights him up
and turns her off
and turns his daughter against him

Looking at Boobs with Aunt Edie

Me and my Aunt Edie are looking
at my parents' wedding album.
My parents are dead, my Aunt Edie
is living with dementia, I'm fifty
and twice divorced—just to give you
an idea, a preamble. On the first page
a photo of my mother and grandmother.
Aunt Edie's short-term memory is shot,
but she can still remember the name
of her 4th grade teacher, her best friend
from camp, her great Aunt Millie, Uncle
Donald, and the exact number of the house
on Observanten Straat where she lived
in Maastricht until she was eight: #26. "Hey,
look how busty Savtah looks," she says,
and we stare awhile at my grandmother's
boobs. I smile, nod, and turn the page
to a photo of my mother and grandfather
walking down the aisle arm-in-arm. "Hey,
look how pointy Reggie's boobs are here,"
says Aunt Edie. And I can't help noticing
the theme that's developing page by page,
breast by breast. And I'm wondering if
this is a side of Aunt Edie that was always
there, only covered up, inhibited, corseted
like her own ample breasts ("which were
always much bigger than your mother's,"
she says to me now) and only coming out
in her late seventies, now that she's forgotten
the reason for keeping it hid. Whatever
the reason, her celebration of the bosoms
of the women of my family is making me
squirm. That's when she looks up, adjusts
her bra strap, fixes me with a penetrating
hazel arrow, and says, "If I didn't know you
better, nephew, I'd say you were blushing."

Orgasms in Autumn

I used to think spring was the sexiest season.
But now I think it's fall
with all its burning smells
and the musculature
of the impatient trees with their
red pants down around their knees
already—and all this talk of peak
foliage, which reminds me of all the talk
of orgasms, which are both the point and
so beside the point. I mean look
how beautiful. I mean feel how impossible—
everything building, everything climbing toward a high
tingling, a ringing in the ears, a flying
down through the world from the highest
branches. When I was a kid
I used to stand with my back to the trunks of trees
(a kind of renunciation
of hide-and-seek) and count
with eyes wide open
the number of leaves falling right now,
then take off running, darting zigzag,
trying to catch them, to take them,
snatch them out of the air mid-dance before
they could touch the ground. I played that game
for hours and hours, years—
sweaty and breathless, happy
just to be catching the falling beauty
in my hands, then letting it go, throwing it back
into the world.

Get Well Card in Cardiology

The beautiful nurses of history
are all out in the corridor,
nursing. If you push the call button
their beautiful voices
will ask you what you want.
If you tell them you want *them*
they will give you their beautiful
laughter and a gentle
rebuke. If you keep on pushing the call button
they will send in the plain nurses
whose voices are also beautiful
to confuse you. If you close your eyes and just
keep on pushing the call button for all it's worth
they will take the call button away from you.
The world is like that.
What you need is one of those crazy great ideas
men get when they're in love,
the kind that just might work,
the kind that makes a man great
and gets him the woman. History
is full of crazy great ideas. Borrow one.
You can do better than pushing your call button
and pulling your catheter out.
Very mediocre ideas, my friend.
You just keep on imagining all day
every day of your convalescence
the beautiful nurses of history
lining up in the corridor outside your room,
and you will get better soon,
because history is on your side,
and exercising your imagination
is not only good for your heart,
it's good for God and country.
Repeat after me: I pledge allegiance
to beauty.

The Place of Literature

Mr. Gordon was perhaps a little tipsy
at the awards ceremony, perhaps a little
scornful of the football coach's ode
to yardage, the basketball coach's
paeons to the MVPs, the music teacher's touting
her flautist, the science teacher his
scion of Einstein. So when Mr. Gordon
got up to give the literary magazine award
to me, he lurched a little drunkenly, swayed
a little imperceptibly, steeply rocking in his
moment on stage. Not to be outdone,
he said in his opinion I was probably
the greatest poet writing in English anywhere today—
and a gasp went up from the high school auditorium,
then murmurs of admiration and disbelief and
mutiny spread through the audience as I rose
to accept Mr. Gordon's slightly exaggerated
handshake. Then he kissed me on the mouth,
and raised my hand above my head in the manner
of referees and prizefighters, grinning glaringly
over at the football coach, and nodding trochaically.

Italian Cuisine

I'm visiting my half-sister Olga
in Bologna. She's 45 and married
to an Italian. I'm 15, American, and the only
Italian word I know besides spaghetti

is baloney. My family
history reads like one of those libretti
where everyone is falling in love and jumping
out of windows: alleluia, allioop!

My nephew Dario, 4 years older than me (go
figure), takes me to a party on the Via Faenza
where everyone is smoking and eating
pot brownies. They take turns

practicing their English on the American.
I feel famous, then exploited.
Someone is telling a long hilarious joke
in Italian. All of my interpreters

are cracking up and rolling on the floor,
mute with laughter. I smile helplessly,
sweep the floor with my eyes for the dropped
English. It evaporates like water in a pot

of giddy spaghetti. The brownies kick in.
I float to the window, look out at the porticos leapfrogging
to infinity through the streets of Bologna.
I close my eyes and see

Olga in her kitchen, holding a rolling pin;
my father in Prague, holding a cigarette
like a leaky pen, pointing it drippingly up
at a portrait of Jan Masaryk who

jumped (go figure) out a window.
I see Wendy Iazzoni back in Jersey, smiling
at the end of a long tunnel in space—
I can see the gap between her teeth perfectly,

I can even see the gap between the buttons
of her blouse, which was always space enough—
when Dario taps my scapula and we lapse
into English. Back at Olga's

it's rigatoni for dinner—
little fluted tunnels floating
in a white wine sauce. I'm still
stoned. I hold one drippingly up

to my left eye while closing
my right: Olga floats into focus
glaring like the Inquisition at Dario
who's holding a rigatoni telescope

of his own, peering through it across
the dinner table at me, the American
Galileo. "Nevertheless,
it moves," I intone. He explodes

into exorbitant laughter.

Open

I'm open to god but I don't like capitalizing
on god. I mean I'll open the door
to the Jehovah's Witnesses, but I won't
let them dominate the conversation.
"For what profiteth it a man," I ask them,
"if he gains salvation but loses
the remote?" They smile uncomfortably
as I turn and head into the kitchen,
returning with the longest carving knife
in the drawer. Their eyes get very big
and they start back-pedaling toward the door...
"It's a double-edged sword," I tell them,
"this war between the spirit and the flesh."
Then I prostrate myself in front of
the couch, and cast around underneath it
till the knife touches up against something
I hope is the remote. "The way a life of renunciation
touches up against something one hopes
is the soul..." I say to my well-dressed
guests hurtling down my front steps now
two at a time, not hearing me at all,
though my door remains open, my cheek turned
to the cool hardwood floor, and I'm fishing
around for something lost, contemplating all this dust.

God, Dan

I was a junior and Dan was a senior
drug addict in the school of arts and sciences. Neil
Young was a prolific songwriter with no
allegiances, except for the music. I had never
done cocaine before, so while he was cutting it
on the square mirror on top of the dresser, I put on
the record and asked him what kind of shape
I would be in for class at two o'clock. He said
it was an aphrodisiac, so go figure. He was
cutting class himself and meeting his girlfriend
at one-thirty, because all it made him want to do
was fuck. I didn't have a girlfriend. I had a Comparative
Religion class at two o'clock, and now I was thinking
twice about getting high before God and
man. But Dan was in a hurry, and he handed me
the rolled-up twenty which I knew enough to
stick inside my nose and aim at the nearest
cloud-row reflected in the square lake on top
of the dresser—and sniff vigorously. Then Dan
was saying something about making love
as he left the room, and Neil was saying something
about needing someone to love him the whole
day through, and I was alone with God and no one
to talk to about God, when the coke kicked in.
Thank God for Dan, who came back looking
for his twenty. "I don't think God created the world,"
I said to him as he scooped up the bill and licked
the top of the dresser with his tongue, as an afterthought.
"In fact, I doubt He even knows we're here."
"Thank God for that," said Dan, "because all I want
to do in the world is snort cocaine and rub my cock."
I loved his honesty. I told him I would try to weave it in
to my paper on Abraham. "You need to get laid, man,"
said Dan. "Old man, take a look at my life," said Neil.
I sat down at the typewriter and began: "'Here am I,'
said Abraham to God." "I'm out of here," said Dan.

The Self

It was a Buddhist lecture on the Self.
There must have been fifty people
in that room with the eight Vicissitudes,
six Stages of Metta, four Noble Truths,
three Kinds of Suffering and two
ceiling fans spinning, spinning. She was
sitting on the other side of the room,
touching herself. I couldn't help staring.
She was twisting a strand of her long hair
round her fingers absent-mindedly
while listening to the speaker, holding it up
to her lips, sniffing it, tasting it,
eyeing it doubtfully, then letting it go.
She caressed her cheek, her forehead,
the palm of her hand cupped her chin, fingers
drumming. It was a pensive attitude
lasting only a moment, for her hands
grew restless again, and she started hugging
herself, her left hand massaging her right
shoulder, her right hand making excursions
to the hip, belly, armpit where it moored itself
with a thumb camped out on the small hillock
of her left breast. I couldn't help wondering
if she could feel my eyes on her body the way I could
feel her hands on her body on mine. "Don't
attach to anything as *me* or *mine*," the Buddhist
speaker who was Jewish before he was Buddhist
was saying, "because attachment is the second
arrow." That's when I realized I had missed
what the first arrow was. And then, as in a dream,
I was trying to raise one of my hands lying
in my lap like two dead birds, belly-up, to ask.

The Conversations of Men

My girlfriend says she would like to be a fly
on the wall between two urinals.
What would she overhear? she asks me.
I tell her the last time a man spoke to me
above a urinal, I think he said, "How about them Bruins?"
And what did you say in return? she wants to know.
I say I didn't know what to say because
I don't know anything about hockey,
and I didn't watch the game or even know
there was one. But I didn't want him
to know that. So I think I said, "Goddamn!"
because it sounded heartfelt yet noncommittal,
because he may or may not have been a Bruins fan,
and because the Bruins may or may not have won,
and because he was trying to make contact
with his gender, and if I said I didn't see the game,
or if I said I didn't follow hockey or don't
give a shit about the Bruins, he would probably
feel like he hadn't made contact. And I would feel
less of a man. So I said, "Goddamn!" and he said
"Unbelievable!" and shook his head in approval,
or maybe it was disapproval—it was hard to tell, I tell her,
because the whole thing was more or less peripheral.

Cholera

In the dream you said, "I love
this time of day—it's called the cholera."
I said I thought the cholera was a disease.
You said, "It is a disease but it's also
a time of day." There was no dictionary
in the dream, and we were sitting outside
at a café or a hospital. You asked if I'd read
Love in the Time of Cholera, and I said
I started it once, but never got past the first
50 pages. And you said, "That explains it."
I wondered if you meant the book explains
the time of day you love and why it's called
the cholera; or if you meant something else,
something about me and the way I am, namely,
one who can't get past the first 50 pages
of a book you love. Which would mean
something else entirely. And then I said
"I think cholera is one of those words that,
if divorced from its meaning, would make a beautiful
name for a girl. Like Treblinka." You gave me
a pained look in the dream then, and I wondered
if it meant you didn't agree with me or if it meant
that what you were eating didn't agree with you.
Either way, it was plain to see that you were suffering.

Poetry at the Burger King

Where is it? It's not here.
All these plastic chairs and tables
are empty. Nothing but a lot of
dead meat here, and this associate
behind the counter mumbling: *Welcome
to Burger King, may I take your order?*
Mine is the only car outside in the sad
parking lot ringed by a handful
of gimpy trees, a blue dumpster in the corner.
Beyond that, the highway where I
came from, and where I will return.
If your daily life seems poor, said Rainer
Maria Rilke, do not blame *it*. Blame yourself.
Tell yourself you are not poet enough
to call forth its riches. I'm fingering a salty
corner of my empty French fries pocket,
licking my fingers, looking out the window
and telling myself I am not poet enough,
when I notice two kids running, sort of
galloping, sort of hopscotching across
the sad parking lot ahead of their parents
and into the Burger King. They are
very happy to be here, this little girl and boy,
jumping up and down now at the counter,
dancing to the song of the associate
which wasn't a song until their dancing
made it so. There are so many riches
on the menu, they can't make up their minds.
And while their parents order they play
duck duck goose, touching all the tables
and all the chairs, the girl behind the boy,
following him, copying him and laughing
louder and louder, because it's all so wonderful
here at the Burger King, which they seem to have
all to themselves, except for one man in a booth
smiling, writing something down on a piece of paper.

Boy with Father with Foreign Accent

My father's name is Egon,
pronounced *egg* on.
He grew up in Czechoslovakia
so he pronounces a lot of his words

wrong. I help him with that and in turn
he helps me spell Czechoslovakia.
I'm the only kid in my class who can.
I'm writing it now on the placemat

at the International House of Pancakes.
We're international, me and Egon,
sitting across from each other in our booth
like nations at the table. A language

is a dialect with an army, so I drill him
in the names of all the syrups, and he
drills me in C-z-e-c-h-o-s-l-o-v-a-k-i-a
while we wait for my pancakes and his eggs.

"Egg on your face," I say to him,
and he reaches for a napkin.
"It's just an expression," I explain,
and he asks me what it means. I say

I'm not sure, but whenever I hear it
it makes me think of him. "You have Egon
on your face," he says. And I patiently
correct him. But he says again, "You have

Egon on your face—you have my nose
and mouth and chin. Egon on your face—
and you can't wipe him off."

Miracles

Spiritual texts are the most boring books in the world.
None of them mentions a bicycle
or a Ferris wheel, or baseball, or sea lions, or ice cream.
They just lump them all together into "the world."
The "world of appearances." The "world of illusions."
You can walk through this world and not
believe it for a minute. You can get to the end of it
and not believe that either. The miracle is seeing
right through the world to another
world that's right here, right now.
But you have to let go of everything.
You have to let go of everything—you can
start by letting go of these words, just let them
go. Let them fall through the air, skim
your knee, spill to the floor. How to read these words
when they're lying on the floor face-down
like bodies? That is the seeming difficulty.
You can sit in a small room all alone with your body
and not believe it for a minute. You can
don the humble johnny that closes in the back,
and when the doctor comes in with his numbers,
which are your numbers, you can
not believe them either. You can let them fall from his lips,
skim your ear, pool on the floor where your eyes
and his eyes have fallen. He won't
mention the bicycle or the Ferris wheel, which is
taking up a lot of room right now in the little
examining room where a sea lion has clambered up
onto the table and is barking, and the baseballs are flying,
and the vendors are hawking ice cream—because he can't
see them. He can't perform a miracle.

Waiting Room

The woman with the portable oxygen tank
is standing in front of the exotic fish tank
looking at the fish. The woman looks like the fish
with her bulging eyes and yellow raincoat and exotic
portable oxygen tank. The fish tank is
too small for the fish, thinks the woman. If only
it were bigger, she could breathe easier.
The fish swim back and forth, back and forth,
looking for the way out. They think there is one.
They think if they keep looking they will find it.
Death is the only way out of the exotic fish tank,
thinks the woman. The dead ones are lifted out
by a living hand, which the fish probably think
is the long hand of Death. It scares them and they
scatter. But it's the same hand that feeds them,
this hand that lifts them gently up when they are
no more. It cares for them. It loves them. It would
hold them to itself, if only they could be held and
live. But they can't, thinks the woman, looking down
at the small bones of her own hand, and lifting it up
to adjust her breathing tube, inhales jaggedly, floats away.

Frame

If you framed some photos of people you don't know
and put them up on your mantelpiece and piano,
on your desk and dresser and end tables,
or just hung them on all the walls—you'd be surrounded
by pictures of smiling people you would probably
never meet in your life, faces of total strangers
who nevertheless, over time, would begin to grow
familiar to you, intimate even, strangely, namelessly
known. And if someday, somewhere, somehow
you began to run into them out in the world,
wouldn't it feel like coming home? Wouldn't it feel
like love, the kind of love you only feel for your own
children, whom you love so much it hurts, even now
that they're grown, distant, reticent, strangers almost?

Splinter

Because he felt nothing,
because he felt he couldn't
feel, he felt he couldn't
love, and he lifted
the wooden door of the garage
which housed the car which
housed the easeful death
which he was half in love with,
when a small dark
insidious grace
entered his left palm
near the thumb
and lodged itself there
and he winced in pain,
and let go of his plan,
holding the injured hand
in the uninjured one,
holding it up to his mouth
as though drinking from it,
or eating from it,
or weeping into it,
and in this attitude walked
back into his life.

The Cup

When I find it in the basement
on the shelf above the dryer
under a pile of his old undershirts

I take it down and turn it over
and over, remembering how
uncomfortable he said it was

in spite of the rubber edge
and vent-holes, the plastic shell
shaped to fit a twelve-year-old penis

and testicles, which were being
tested on the football field that first
day at Pop Warner. All the fathers

stood around talking football,
but all I could contribute was,
"Growing up, I played soccer myself..."

Then I was standing a little apart
like a pedestrian looking for my son
in traffic—football helmets and identical

red jerseys in gridlock, and I couldn't
find him. Because I couldn't remember
his number, and they all looked the same

running around out there for the love of
yardage. I felt a little panicky. Technically,
I'd lost him, lost sight of him, and everyone

knows what happens to kids who fall through
the hatches on the football fields of life...
Then I noticed—hanging back in the end zone

all alone—number 26, adjusting his protective
cup. And I kept my eyes on him until
the day he left for college. And finding it now

all these years later, I hold it for a moment
against my own testicles, whence he came. And then
I hold it up to my face, like an oxygen mask.

From
HURT INTO BEAUTY

(FutureCycle Press, 2012)

The Violence of the Violins

It was in them, they would say.
It was what they were, what they
did. It was part of them, carved
into them like an F hole, like
a clef tattooed onto a biceps.
And there was nothing you
could say or do to change that.
It was their way. It was the way
of the world, and also of the sun
exploding a million miles away,
warming your soft cheek. Face
the music, they would say. Stop
listening with your eyes closed.
See the string tightened almost
to breaking, the bow torturing it
into song. Feel the skin stretched
over the drum so tightly it makes
your heart pound. And where
did you think it all came from,
the easy melody, the high tinkling
finery? We are hurt into beauty.
And you, up in the balcony, rising
to your feet, applauding fiercely, look
down at what your own hands are doing.

The Names

I want to say something about the names—
Ahmed, Fuad, Tarek, Toufic—
that are in the news these days—
Yusif, Anwar, Umar, Ismael—
and the way the newscasters have had
to practice pronouncing them. Abdul, Amar, Abu,
Muqtada al-Sadr. Don't you just
love saying, "Muqtada al-Sadr?"
If you lined up all the names and just
said them, one after the other,
it would sound like you were fluent
in Arabic. You could pull one over
on your friends down at the pub:
lubricate your tongue with a few beers,
then turn to Geoff or Bill or Steve, and say,
"Muqtada al-Sadr Ahmed Fuad
Abdul Abu Umar Muhammed," and just
wait for a reaction. Chances are
a painful silence would swallow the pub whole,
because everyone would think you had been praying,
or reciting a poem, or a fatwa, when in fact
all you were doing was saying the names,
just lining them up and one by one
firing off those frighteningly beautiful names.

Concentration Camps

The way I explained it to myself, the way
I made sense of it in my own way (I was eight
when I first learned about them), was all those people
starving and crying and dying together in those big
piles behind the barbed wire—were forced to concentrate
on suffering. So it made sense to call it that. That part
made sense, I thought, because concentration was very
difficult. And I hated having to do it myself
in elementary school when the teacher caught us
looking out the window at the trees, or the sky, or the rooftops
of the houses across the street—when she caught us looking
out at life—and forced us cruelly back to the problem
under our noses, the problem of the numbers, the problem
that wasn't going away no matter how much we
looked away from it. And those people, I thought, they must have
tried looking away from it too. They must have groaned
and looked away, and there must have been sky
above them, and trees on the other side, and maybe even a red
rooftop or two off in the distance where life was going on
in rooms with clean white linen and tinkling forks and knives...
The way you make sense of a problem like that, a solution like that,
a number like that, a number that's so big you can't fit it
in your head, can't fit it in the world—though the world keeps trying
that solution, over and over—is to break it down, like the teacher
said, and keep breaking it down until you get to the smallest parts,
the ones divisible only by themselves and one: sky, tree, house,
one little boy. Then look out the window at the world again
and see if it looks any different.

The First Day

They found the perpetrators.
The ones who committed those unspeakable acts.
Acts that were so unspeakable
they were all over the news,
so we all heard about them
and could only cover our mouths
and wonder how such people could do such things.
They found them, and they arrested them,
and they tried them, and found them guilty. And the judge,
who was a very wise judge,
pronounced sentence: Begin again.
They must all begin again. Go back
and learn again the things we learned as children,
things they either never learned in the first place
or else somehow unlearned in the unspeakable
unforgiving place the world has always been
and will always be.
Things about being
with other people, about sharing, and keeping
your hands to yourself,
and laying your head down on your desk
in the crook of your elbow.
And so they were remanded
to kindergarten, each to a different
kindergarten, so they couldn't sit next to each other
and scoff, and keep each other from learning.
On the first day
each was brought in in shackles
before the bell rang,
and made to sit in one of the tiny desks,
so his knees came up to his chin. And when the children arrived
they noticed him right away, and gathered around him
timidly, curiously, a few emboldened to ask
questions, the kinds of questions only children
will ask: Are those real handcuffs? Are you
our new teacher? Are you Miss Butler's boyfriend?
And one of them climbed up into his lap, and one of them
rested a small hand on his huge shoulder,
and one, a girl, gazed up long and searchingly
into his dark, flitting, downcast eyes.

Clutch Steal

"This John Havlicek, he is Czech,"
says my father who is Czech
and doesn't speak English all that well
and doesn't know what a lay-up is, or a free-throw,
or a pick. We are sitting on the paisley couch,
watching the Celtics play the 76ers. It's 1965.
I hate to tell him, I tell him
as I steal the bag of potato chips from him,
but John Havlicek isn't Czech.
He's from Ohio. Born and raised. My father
was visiting someone in Belgium
when the Nazis invaded Czechoslovakia—
someone who set a pick for him, someone
who saw it all coming—and he escaped
to Paris, then to Lisbon, then to Oslo,
then to New York. Always one step ahead.
He was lucky. He was more than lucky.
He was—what's the word in English?—
charmed. And he lived. He lived, unlike his own
father, and mother, and brothers and sisters—his entire
team. All lost by the time that nightmare
was over. Twenty years later, he's sitting with me
on a paisley couch in a house in New Jersey,
watching the Celtics play the 76ers,
the announcer's impossible English sprinkled
with Havliceks: "Havlicek for two." "Havlicek
from the corner." "Havlicek under the boards."
And then John Havlicek steals the ball—
a clutch steal in the closing seconds of that game,
clinching the Eastern Conference Championship
and immortalizing Havlicek forever. My father
steals the potato chips back and says, "I am
liking this John Havlicek. He is maybe
from Ohio. But he is Czech. And he is charmed."

The Giving Tree

My Aunt Hannah taught 2nd grade.
And after the first amputation
which was only a couple of toes
on her left foot, she came
to school carrying a silver cane,
and she let the kids use it
as a prop in their little skits,
and as a stickball bat at recess,
and to reach up into the tree
to rescue the kite. And the kids
were happy. But after the second
and third and fourth amputations—
this little piggy and his neighbor,
then the whole damn block, then up to the knee,
and then a year later all over again
on the other side of the street—
the kids had a different teacher.
And my Aunt Hannah came to school
in a silver wheelchair, and she let the kids
push her around in it. And some of them
sat in her lap as she read to them
at reading time. And they asked her
questions, unselfconsciously, the way
only kids will ask: What happened
to your legs? Where are the legs now?
How do you take a shower? How
do you drive a car? It was not unlike
show-and-tell, and my Aunt Hannah
was happy to answer. She even joked a little,
and slapped one stump and then the other,
so it looked like a flam on a pair of bongos,
or a rim shot after the punch line
of a bad joke in the Catskills.

Throwing Snowballs at Cars

From our little redoubt
up on the hill
we lobbed our redoubtable

arsenal of white
handcrafted ordnance
one by one over the hedges

and listened
for the gratifying
thunk

on the roofs and hoods of the passing
innocents
who mostly just kept trundling dumbly

along
through the purely perfect-for-packing
driven snow. But once

an innocent in a beat-up pickup
stopped. And stayed there. Idling. Fuming.
We froze. Our fingers and toes

twitching. Our hearts racing. Our noses
running. Finally he drove off, but he doubled
back around, and routed our little

redoubt. And there's no doubt
he would have beaten the shit out of us
if he caught any of us—

but we dispersed
like a burst snowball ourselves
and melted into the neighborhood

like so many scared shitless
snowflakes, no two of us exactly
repentant.

Schadenfreude

"Leave it to the Germans," said Ben.
"They didn't invent it," I said. "They just named it."
"To name a thing is to own it," he said. "It's theirs."
And he walked away then,

waving goodbye with his
back to me, airily, triumphantly, the argument
won, the conversation over as
far as he was concerned. Though I don't

dislike Ben exactly, nor envy him his
wife or Ph.D., which is in poetry—
the wife very pretty, beautiful even—when
a month later he tells me she told him she wants

out, I can't help feeling—not joy
exactly, I wouldn't call it *Freude*—
not the sort of feeling you'd write an ode to,
but more the sort you might

write a dark little conversational piece
in quatrains about—
just to say the conversation isn't over
until it's over.

Pleasure

When you're in pain
you take
pleasure in nothing
but pain's
diminishment,
if pleasure
you can call it,
testing
the thinness of it,
disbelieving,
distrusting,
tiptoeing
down into the kitchen
where a few dirty dishes
that aren't yours
wait in the sink,
and you begin
washing them
slowly,
thoroughly,
gratefully,
the warm
water on your wrists,
the sweet-
smelling soap, the clean
dishes stacking
in the dish rack,
dripping,
glistening,
solid.

Escape Artist

I've always wanted to be
excused. From the table.
From school. From work.
From life, actually.
I don't feel well, may I be
excused from feeling?
I've always wanted to get
out of things. Downright
Houdiniesque. I'd like
to get out of this body. I don't
remember how I got in.
I'd like to go by climbing
your body. Down your body and out
of my body. I think that's how
we get here in the first place.
I don't remember the first place.
I'd like to go back there though.
Excuse me if I elbow,
shoulder, knee. Excuse me if I
worm my way out of the crowded
now. We either go by breaking
into blossom, or by wilting
in place, the latter being so
heartbreaking, you have to look
away. You have to look away.

Leveling the Playing Field

Before they leveled the playing field
one side was always running uphill,
which was hard. And the other side
was always running downhill, which was
hard too—hard to stop the ball from rolling,
hard to stop yourself from running
when you're running down a hill after a ball.
Downhill had certain advantages though.
It was true. But uphill had advantages too—
you could belay; you could stick a strategic
foot out, trip a careening downhill guy
mid-stride. And anyway, we usually
switched at halftime. So when the referees
came up with the idea, we scratched our heads
and tried to envision a playing field that was
level. "You mean get rid of the hill?" we asked
incredulously. They nodded vehemently
and their excellent silver whistles hanging
on lanyards round their necks bobbed in sympathy.
The bulldozers and the backhoes arrived
the next day, the tines of their buckets biting
into our hill, eating it away before our eyes,
and before we could say time out, or foul play,
or off sides—which some of us did say, although
by then it was too late—they'd gone and changed
the game forever. Some of us quit outright, preferring
to sit in judgment up in the stands—the closest
thing to a hill that they had. And some of us kept on playing,
adapting ourselves to the changing landscape,
learning the new steps, and the new names, making
new friends, many of whom were so young that
they'd never played on a hill. They could only
imagine, they said. They could only shake their heads
and regard us in a squinting sort of way, as though
the sun were going down behind a hill, behind us.

People in Deaf Houses

Here's the church and here's the steeple.
The deaf people have barricaded the doors,
hot-wired the school buses, moved them
in front of the gates, and let the air out of the tires.
They've shut the campus down, and the police
can't do anything about it, because they don't
know sign language. And neither does the president
of the college. And neither does the chairman of the board
of trustees, and neither do the trustees themselves.
The trustees can't be trusted with this college, this
church, this school, this blessed sacrament.

In the deaf world, deaf is good. Deaf people marry
other deaf people, and live in deaf houses,
and do not throw deaf carpenters' telephone numbers
away, but give them to other deaf homeowners
looking for a good deaf carpenter, because deaf
is a good and trusted name all over the deaf world.

Here's the hospital and here's the urology unit.
Open the door and see all the doctors
with their deft fingers and expensive educations.
Here is one performing a vasectomy
on a deaf patient who has elected to have it
because he doesn't want any children.
And the surgeon has a slight accent, maybe
German. And the sign language interpreter
has a professional code of ethics,
and is signing what the surgeon is saying
but not what the interpreter is thinking
about German-speaking surgeons and vasectomies,
about Aryans and eugenicists and the forced
sterilizations of the congenitally deaf
in Europe only 40 years ago, about the protests
going on right now at Gallaudet, and about
cochlear implants being performed in this very
hospital, on deaf children who haven't elected to have them.

Alexander Graham Bell invented the telephone.
He was a teacher of the deaf. He had a deaf mother,
and a deaf wife, too. And he knew
that deaf people marry other deaf people

and live in deaf houses. And he deplored that fact.
He deplored deaf people. He urged Congress to act,
to prohibit deaf marriages, to reduce the risk
of more deaf babies. He wasn't a Hitler
or an Eichmann exactly. He didn't advocate
killing the deaf. He loved the deaf. He taught the deaf.
He was only trying to eradicate the deaf
for their own good. For the good of the world.

Here's the church and here's
the steeple. The deaf students are burning
their oppressors in effigy. They're saying: *Look!*
To anyone with eyes to see, they're saying: *Look!*
And the interpreter's fingers are flying,
and the surgeon's fingers are snipping, and the nurse is
adjusting the light above the deaf patient
lying on the table with his johnny hiked up, his little
deaf penis the center of attention. And the interpreter
who has been trying all this time not to look at it,
looks at it. Takes a good long look.

Homophobia

I have a friend who is hydrophobic—
he wants to learn how to swim
but he is too afraid
of the water
to give himself over to it
and just float.

And I have another friend who
is agoraphobic—he wants
to see the world,
and to see the country,
and to see the big city,
but he's too afraid
to come out
of his tiny apartment
which is a closet really.

And my claustrophobic friend would love
to take the elevator,
my gephyrophobic friend wishes
she could drive over bridges
instead of having to go all the way around
each morning to get to work
and each night to get home again
before finally lying down
next to the one she loves.

One-and-Twenty

When I was fifty-one with that kind of insomnia
where you wake up earlier and earlier
and drink lots of coffee and write
lots of poetry, my son was just nineteen
with that home-from-college-for-the-summer
kind of mania, where you go to bed later
and later, and sleep until two in the afternoon.
The drinking age in America was one-and-twenty.
A. E. Housman was a classical scholar
who wrote lots of poetry about doomed youth
in the English countryside. No use talking
to a lad of nineteen about waiting two years
before starting to drink, especially when
he's already learned how up in college. Housman
taught at a college in London, and later at a college
in Cambridge. One night we passed each other—me
and the lad—like two sleepless ship captains in a dark
kitchen at four in the morning. I was heading
for the coffee. He was heading for the toilet.
I could smell the booze on his breath from across
the ages. "Dad," he said, "I can't believe you
get up this early—what time is it, anyway?"
"Son," I said, like a refrain, "I can't believe you
are getting home this late. It's four o'clock in the morning!"
Then we both sailed silently on in our opposite
directions, with our opposite wakes. But a few
minutes later, sipping my coffee and scratching
out a line, then putting it back again, I sensed him
hovering tipsily in the doorway, steeply rocking.
"I love you, man," he said, a little drunkenly.
And I knew enough of love, and I knew enough
of poetry, and I knew enough of sobriety to know
he meant it more than he could say sober. "I love you, too,
man," I said, gave the boy a kiss, and put him to bed.

Dear Hallmark

I know some kids who'd rather make their own.
And I know some grownups who would rather
cut their own tongues out
than let you speak for them. Helplessly intelligent
surrealists, glib intellectuals, haiku bicyclists, some
of my best friends. But I'll give you this, you have
sold more poems than all the moderns and postmoderns
put together. And the people love you. Are the people just
stupid? Are the poets just jealous? Are the pharmacists
just high on life? The truth is, I love your timeless
earnestness. I do. In sickness and in health. Births and deaths
and all occasions in between. Because it goes without saying—
the whole world goes without saying. Saying doesn't
make it go. Never did and never will. But you,
you say without going, like the clock that doesn't
go, the clock that stays the same, your hands always
together, in applause, or prayer, or shared joy, or sorrow where
you can only wring your hands, fumble for the words,
and say the words are inadequate. Which, of course, they are.
But at least you say them. You say them for us when we go
without saying, and when we go without knowing
what to say, or don't go at all but send you stammering
in our stead. And here I stand in your aisle, in your
shadow, in your presence, my hands in my pockets, fumbling
for my wallet, feeling like I'm in the presence of
not greatness, not brilliance, not scholarship or virtuosity,
but love. I am in the presence of love here, helplessly
simple, deliberately compassionate, practicing forever
its imperfect loopy cursive with its pink tongue sticking out.

Hegemony

Three of my cousins are deaf.
But I have lots of cousins,
so the deaf ones
were always in the minority
at family gatherings
where they'd commandeer a couch
or the kitchen table and juggle
their hands. It was a language
the rest of us didn't understand
because we never bothered to learn it.
Their conversations and our conversations
sailed along contiguously
like ships passing in the night
or like an English frigate passing
over a Deaf submarine during
détente. One by one they got married
to three deaf spouses. So then there were six.
And one of them ended up having
two deaf children. So then there were eight.
Eventually they all divorced
and remarried other deaf people
with deaf stepchildren and deaf exes
and deaf in-laws and deaf
cousins. And before we knew it
we were totally outnumbered
at the family gatherings
and consigned to a corner
of the sectional, whispering
and ducking the flying hands,
feeling rather small
and blind, like moles or voles
trembling in the shadows
of the raptors.

Half Moon

The two chairs
that we sat in

this morning
in our pajamas

in the sunny
kitchen

kissing

are still in the same
position

this evening
when I get home

in the dark
I sit in

one
then the other

Her Ear

He loved her ear
literally. Not
the figurative ear—
not the sensitivity
to music or poetry
which she arguably
didn't possess—
but her literal ear.
Its pinna and lobe.
Its cartilaginous-
ness. He loved
to take it in his mouth
and bite it tenderly,
lovingly. And he loved
looking into her brown eyes
which took the world in
literally, and shone
with a happiness
that was brown as earth
with flecks of green.

Passive Voice

It is given to me
is the passive they're parsing
in linguistics class.

He's the sign language interpreter
for a deaf student making
eyes at him

and noise with her corn chips'
plastic wrapper.
She's tonguing a corn chip

and wrinkling her nose
which she knows he knows
means *ooh salty,*

and telling him in
no uncertain terms,
It is given to you.

Sometimes it happens
that way, love
just lands in your lap,

starts conjugating itself
in the second person
singular.

He will ask her to marry him,
to give up linguistics,
come live with him in

a house in the suburbs
among the Thickly
Settled signs.

Here's the church
and here's the steeple.
The deaf people will sit

where they can see
the sign language interpreter.
They will name their first child

Vowel, after
the dilating mouth
of pleasure;

they will fill their home
with the tongues of a hundred
speechless lives:

the plosives of fish
browsing the fishbowl,
the shrugging shoulders

of the spider plants,
the noiseless stutter
of candles.

It's all just tremblingly
achingly waiting
to be

received.

Fledgling

My training wheels lie in the grass
like legs. My father stands over them,
steadying the bicycle with one hand
while with the other he beckons
with a grimy finger. A Philips-head
sticks in the earth beside the severed
pair. The whole scene looks like an amputation.
I will never walk again, if I can help it—
as soon as I learn how to fly. Flying
will be a little like dying, and a little
like being born. I mount the bike
which wobbles slightly in my father's grip
the way the earth wobbles in the grip
of the late afternoon sun going down
behind the huddled houses. The seat
which is a little higher than the sun,
and the handlebars which are approximately
two stars, together form my north and south poles.
My spine is the prime meridian. My nose
sticks out over the top of the hill, on top
of the world, sniffing the air for the bottom.

Light Bulb

"I wanna be an inventor
like Thomas Lava Edison," he says,
erupting from the dinner table
and trailing a white dinner napkin

and leaving his untouched mashed potatoes
in the shape of a volcano,
the gravy cooling inside the crater
left by the beaked ladle.

After the chuckling dishwasher dies down,
I press my ear to the door of his
laboratory, and I hear his small voice
asking questions and also

answering. Soon he reappears with
two toy cars, a red one and a blue,
parks them on the dining room table,
installs himself in a chair—my chair—

and bids me sit. The demonstration begins:
"I've invented a talking car horn, Dad.
With a menu. You choose from the things *you* always say
when people cut you off, or move too slow,

or don't put on their blinkers. Only *now*
they'll be able to hear you." The cars start up:
VROOM, VROOM. The red one shouts:
"Come on, wake up, buddy. Sometime this

century would be nice." The blue replies: "Relax,"
and turns left. The red continues straight: "Nice
turn signal, jerk." He looks up at me with
eyes as big as headlights. "Would you

buy it?" he asks as the cars fly up
and out in opposite arcs above his head,
grind to a halt midair, upside down in his hands.

From
NAMING NAMES

(Main Street Rag, 2013)

Fame

I used to wonder what it felt like
to be David Mitnik
who had hair under his arms already
in the 6th grade. More specifically,
I wondered if one could feel the hair there—
if one had hair there—
or was it more like the hair on your head
which you can't really feel
unless the sun is beating down on it or the rain
has soaked it through, and then, arguably,
it's the rain or sun you feel and not the hair
per se. But the hair that grew
where the sun didn't shine—now that
I knew nothing about at the famous
tender age of twelve and a half. I didn't
want to *be* David Mitnik, I just wanted
something like an autograph—
what might rub off of his signature
armpit hair by being in his presence,
on his team, or even in his chair in his absence.
I remember once when he was absent
I sat down at his desk—still warm, it seemed,
from so much precociousness—
and I imagined myself in his skin,
the hair crowding my seat like
a crowd in their seats, each individual
tendril standing up and cheering, doing the wave, rooting
for puberty! Which finally came, of course,
but it grew old fast. And it wasn't long
before I ached to return to the obscure
vacant lots of childhood
where nothing much grew
and the old games ruled
and the smooth balls flew.

Boxy Poem for Mr. Beck

Mr. Beck taught gym and sex education
back when there wasn't a curriculum per
se. So he mostly punted in the classroom,
relating blow-by-blow what he and his wife
had done the night before. It was x-rated
and educational. You had to hand it to him
for thinking outside the box that was our
classroom; the box that was our high school;
the box that was our life in small town USA.
In gym we all did fifty push-ups while Beck
walked among us, shirtless, like a gardener
coaxing a crop of calisthenic chrysanthemums
pushing up. He praised the virtue of the push-up,
said you could do them anywhere, anytime.
He said he did them all the time in his office
between classes, in his bedroom between sex
with his wife, and for all he knew he would
be doing push-ups in his coffin after he died.
We could tell just by looking at his pecs that
he wasn't bullshitting us. For all he knew we
didn't love Mr. Beck. But we dearly believed him.

Science

We are doing the Periodic Table
of Elements and Mia got Aluminum.
I wanted Aluminum. I'm mad at Mia
for taking Aluminum when she didn't
even want it. Not the way I did.
I really, really wanted Aluminum.
Because I like its name and its atomic
number, which is 13. Instead I got Boron
which is boring and rhymes with "moron"
and I just know somebody is going to
think of that. And everybody has to fit
their Element on an 8 × 5 index card,
with its name and chemical symbol
and atomic number on the front, and the story
of how it got discovered or isolated
on the back. Aluminum's chemical symbol
is Al, which looks like A-one, like A-plus
one. But Boron's chemical symbol is just B
which is blah, and its atomic weight is 11
which is the age of my older brother Josh
who's mean. And on top of everything Kelsey
got Carbon which is so unfair because
her father drills oil wells for a living
and she's already like the most popular girl
in the whole school and she lives in a big
house on a hill and I hate science now
because it's so random and it really makes
absolutely no sense at all.

Feeling Sorry for the Presidents

I remember Nixon getting up in front of
my mother and father in 1974
and looking so earnest and guilty
that you had to feel sorry for the guy—I mean
I did. I didn't know what he'd done but
whatever it was, I knew my parents wouldn't
forgive him for it any time soon.
I could tell by the way they flicked
the TV off and left the room that Nixon
was grounded for life if my parents
had anything to say about it. I remember
turning the TV back on and feeling
closer to Nixon then, for he reminded me
a little of myself. But now, years later, with Nixon
gone and my parents gone and George W
getting up on TV in front of everyone
and not telling the truth, he looks so
earnest and guilty and he doesn't have
a good vocabulary either—I bet he never
reads books just for the pleasure
of reading them—that I can't help feeling
sorry for the guy. I mean everybody's mad at him
for the big mess he made, and there he stands
in the middle of that mess, with all the bodies
piling up—all the arms and legs and heads—
and he has to say something, but he can't
say what he has to say. He can't say it.

Ten or So

My best friend's older sister Jill
answers the door. "He's not
here come on in." It's just
her and the dog, a kind of poodle cum
retriever that resembles Jill
in a way I can't or don't want to
put my finger on. It follows us
doggily into the den where we sit
down on the lime couch, collapses
in front of us on the floor, panting.
I cross my legs. "So when
is he coming home?" No answer.
Eyes on the dog, she unbuttons
first the second and then the third
of ten or so buttons on her blouse. "It's hot
in here." And then the fourth.
And then the fifth. She's at the age
where she bears her new breasts
like pert little deities seeking
rightful homage. I'm at the age
where I still say "and a half" after
my age. Because I want the full
credit. But today I haven't got
a clue. I stare straight ahead at the wall,
taking in peripherally the pink
dangle of the dog's tongue, the pale
half breast that Jill has bared
down to the pink nipple. I can feel her,
febrile, panting, burning a hole
in the side of my face as I look
away, for the life of me. The life of me.

Fucking

I can still see the pharmacist's face
as he sized me up at the register
and fished the Trojans out from under
all that camouflage of candy
piled on top like a piebald football team
in Troy, then counseled me with a wink, "Don't
mix *these* up with those." I was fifteen, a freshman
on an errand. Faith was much older, a senior
expert on the hydraulics of the penis
of her ex-boyfriend, Mark Winkles, whom
she forsook for my more literary point of view.
But I only ended up disproving
every borrowed theory of hydraulics
that between the two of us
I couldn't come up with
that terrified, truant, spring afternoon
we were scheduled to *do* it. "Fucking,"
Faith had warned me three months earlier,
speaking from her vast singular experience,
"is very intense. We're going to have to
prepare you for this." But our preparations
amounted to her talking about it all the time
which only served to undermine
my confidence. Under the leadership of Epeios
the Greeks built their wooden horse
in three days, which allowed them finally to enter Troy.
For three whole months Faith built up "fucking"
to the point where I was totally
psyched out. When the time finally came,
I couldn't get it up. I couldn't get the Trojan on.
And I couldn't get inside Faith, who finally, quietly
gave up, and went back to Mark Winkles,
leaving me in ruins, scarred for life.
But what I want to know is,
is this a classic story
or an atypical one?

All These Things

"We have a *buttload* of catching up to do,"
says my friend from the second grade
in the first

e-mail that comes out of the cyber
blue. It's a large amount, possibly
a variant of *boatload*. I don't

recognize his name at first. And it's 108
imperial gallons, from the Middle-English
butt: a large

container or cask used for storing
liquids, especially wine. "We sure
do," I write back and click

SEND. He writes about his life, wife, kids, kids'
colleges. And it's more than a person can hold
in two hands, possibly

from the large size of some women's behinds.
I'm clean and sober one day at a time, twice
divorced,

horny, peevish, bookish, parsimonious
with words, and disinclined to give him
mine. My replies

grow smaller and more distant in inverse
proportion to his long and sunny ones,
like a retrograde moon

of Pluto. Then die out altogether. And it's
a surprisingly large amount of contraband
that a customs agent might find

hidden in someone's rectum. It's all
these things. And the bus driver's name
was Karl. The school nurse

was Mrs. Knapp.

To A Writer

I love your verbs.
I love your adverbs.
I love your abs.
The musculature
of your guts.
I hate your guts.
You send me
to the dictionary,
which I love.
The way your I's
reflect
my own deepest
darkest first person
is uncanny.
I can't get you out of
your short stories
and into my poem.
But I can try.
I love your choices.
The way they ripple,
and push
every edge.
The way they branch
and brachiate.
Each choice like
a horse chestnut
with its own pair
of seed-leaves inside,
like testicles,
containing whole
forests.

Reading Sharon Olds

I wonder how her husband feels
about his penis being all over her poems,
especially the earlier poems where
his penis was in its prime, her pen
was on fire, her nose for the poem
was sniffing the poem out uncannily
in every room in the house. Me, I'd
be tickled to have my penis appear
in a poem by Sharon Olds. In fact,
I sort of wonder what it would be like
to be making love to Sharon Olds
now that Sharon Olds is old and her
husband's penis appears less and less
in the poems. Last night I fell asleep
with her book lying open on my stomach,
a picture of the poet, still beautiful
in her late sixties, on the back jacket just
inches from my penis. And I dreamed
we were walking arm in arm like two old
lovers who were friends now, her children
and my children running ahead like scouts
pointing at something we couldn't make out,
calling impatiently to us, their small voices
like the poems we have yet to write. "Turn
up the heat," she said to me, and I knew
she could be talking about my poems
or she could be talking about my life,
and it would be the same thing because her eyes
were the same eyes, and her mouth was
slightly open, as if to say "kiss me" without
saying it. But I didn't kiss her in the dream,
I left her standing there, and I started running
really, really, really, really fast.

Poem

When I finally figured it out—
you know, life, the whole thing—
I couldn't write it down fast enough,
and I was shaking my head in disbelief,
and smiling at the sheer dumb luck
of each new line revealing itself to me
like a winning scratch ticket, hitting it
big. I mean really big. The kind of big
that comes over you slowly and all at once,
like what it will mean for the rest of your life,
how you won't have to work at it anymore
because everything will be different now
and the same. It was a little scary actually,
and my stomach started to hurt. But the pain
was different now. It was part of the joy.
And the joy was different too because it was
unbelievable. I mean I knew it was true—
I just didn't believe it. And that hurt, too.
Then the old hurt gave way to the new
and suddenly everything rhymed a little.

The Proust Is in the Pudding

So I wake up with this line in my head,
the Proust is in the pudding,
fishtailing around on the surface of a dream,
and I grab it, I just take it, and I run with it
downstairs to the computer
where I enter another kind of dream state
where I'm trying to follow the thread of the line
into the poem, and I'm holding on to the line
for dear life like it's a bungee cord and I'm
bungee jumping through the poem *boing boing*
looking around for the thread which is in here
somewhere, I know it is, I trust it is—
it's like you have to trust the line, and you have to trust
the thread not to break when the line breaks
into another line, and another, and another,
the way the line must, the way the dream
breaks into day, like daybreak, like breakfast, like broken
egg yolks—okay maybe not like broken egg yolks,
maybe the egg yolks are a little forced, maybe
I'll take them out later, and maybe
I'll just put them back in again because
I like my egg yolks broken, and also because
sometimes you can do that in a good poem,
especially if you're trusting in something bigger
than yourself, something bigger than egg yolks,
bigger than Proust and madeleines and all the lost
time in the world. Because if you trust in the line
then you're holding on to the line for dear life like a
pull cord on a parachute, it's like you're
parachuting down through the poem
but at the same time you're floating up
(you can only do this in poetry) in the great hot air balloon
of the poem, standing inside the little wicker basket
with a few passengers, a few good readers,
and Marcel Proust with his own wicker picnic basket
full of madeleines, which is actually your source
of heat, your open flame, pushing the envelope
upward, and powering the buoyant
antique iridescent technology of the poem.

Poem on the Fridge

The refrigerator is the highest honor
a poem can aspire to. The ultimate
publication. As close to food as words
can come. And this refrigerator poem
is honored to be here beneath its own
refrigerator magnet, which feels like a medal
pinned to its lapel. Stop here a moment
and listen to the poem humming to itself,
like a refrigerator itself, the song in its head
full of crisp, perishable notes that wither in air,
the words to the song lined up here like
a dispensary full of indispensable details:
a jar of corrugated green pickles, an array
of headless shrimp, fiery maraschino cherries,
a fruit salad, veggie platter, assortments of
cheeses and chilled French wines, a pink
bottle of amoxicillin: the poem is infectious.
It's having a party. The music, the revelry,
is seeping through this white door.

My Submissions

Maybe this is a guy thing but
when I send out my stuff
when I put my stuff out there
it feels like I'm sewing my seed
it feels like I'm a burst dandelion
and each seed is attached to a pappus of fine hairs
like little parachutes in a wind-aided dispersal
of my submissions over long distances
and maybe this is conceited but
that's the conceit that comes to mind and I think
I'd like to explore it a little further if you don't mind
because dandelions produce their seeds asexually
which is exactly how I produce my submissions
which are sometimes outwardly obscene
and which do contain certain sexual overtones
but are nevertheless asexual by nature
which is to say I don't have sex when I'm making them
though I do like to have sex after they're done
because it's in my nature and because
making them is like compression
it's like trying to compress all this pressure
into the simple figure of a leaf
a floret a tendril
and I need to release all that pressure
that's pushing up through the taproot
when I'm done compressing it into something
that's beautiful and true
and winged
and when I get one in there
when I get that acceptance letter it feels like love
it feels like a love letter and I read it over and over
and sniff it and lick it and put it in my buttonhole or hat
and pretty soon it starts to fade and to droop
and it goes to seed and it just goes to show
that everything is vanity after the seed
because it's not about the seed dispersal
it's about the seed production
it's about the making of the seed
because it never gets better than that

I Say

Let us not decry
the decline of the language,
dude.

Let the grammarians
and librarians
and Shakespearians

shake the tiny spears
of their red pens at us.

Let the letter writers
mourn the death of letter writing.

Let the virtuoso
conversationalists grumble
about their dwindling
number.

Let them all
chill. We still
got a handle
on the verbal, baby.

And the language ain't
dying. It's cooking
with oil.

So I say, let us praise
on our geographic
tongues

this living gumbo,
this fine and thick
delicious and nutritious
mud

whence all the beautiful
and endangered species
spring, sprang,

sprung.

Taking the Cake

The urinal
cake, that deodorizer
thingy: small, white,
hockey puck-
like, lozenge-like,
lemon Italian ice-
like, deceptively
fragrant in the urinal's
sepsis, ultimately
irresistible
to the three-year-old
that you were
when you reached your hand in
to take it
and put it in your mouth
while I stood next to you,
not seeing you
because I was looking
blissfully up
at the dropped ceiling,
peeing
the jumbo regular
coffee of the last
rest stop out in torrents,
exhaling contentedly,
feeling good about
life in general
and you and your beautiful
mother waiting in the car
in particular,
not to mention my perfectly
functioning bladder
emptying itself
the way it should,
which always feels
good no matter how
you cut it.

C. Bowen, Plumber

I like this guy
before we even meet.
He's the only one
who called me back, and then
he wipes his feet
for a very long time
on the mat
before coming inside
with a little bow,
then setting out bravely
for the upstairs bathroom
a few steps behind me,
like a lieutenant
or a constable. I look up
'meticulous' after he leaves
and am startled to find
it comes from fear
in Latin. Because he seemed so
fearless, knowledgeable,
mindful of the whole long
history of flood. He was
a very good listener. "It could be
the spindle in your shower valve,
or it could be something
in the drain assembly," he said
as he drew the bath,
then drew a wrench
from his plumber's belt
and climbed into my tub. His entry
in the yellow pages
was the humblest
of all the plumber ads
with their splashy logos
and trite slogans. It read, simply:
C. Bowen, Plumber,
with a number
that rolled off my fingers
like an arpeggio.

He nailed it in under
an hour. And his bill
which has come in today's mail
like a coda
is simply too beautiful
to contemplate.

Man Praying in a Men's Room

I can tell by the angle of his shoes
that he's kneeling. Plus there's something in the air
like straining. The sibilant hint
of a whisper. No toilet paper either—
I know because I considered sitting down in there
myself, before settling in next door, here
where there's paper, and even half a newspaper.
But the news in the neighboring stall
has gotten my attention. The trouble is
there's no story. Not even a headline.
Just a pair of shoes, toes to the floor
like a ballerina's, and something in the air
like leaping. So I do the neighborly thing,
I make up the story myself because
I haven't written anything all week,
and everywhere I look these days there's construction,
things going up all over. And why not
here? I start to build the story in my head
of my neighbor, praying. I give him
good reasons, grown children, a short
lunch break, bald head, small ears, an enormous
craving—the kind you need a Higher Power
to relieve you of. All of a sudden he sniffs,
then he shifts and his story shifts with him.
He sniffs again, sniffles. A shudder. Unmistakably
he is sobbing. I hold my breath, stare straight ahead at a *fuck*
gouged in the gray door. "Excuse me," says a voice
that sounds like it's drowning, and here's his hand
waving beneath the divider. "Have you got any
toilet paper?" I unravel a generous portion,
for who knows how much he'll be needing?—
my weeping neighbor, builder of cathedrals—
and I donate it wordlessly in a tenuous scroll.

Alliteration

I whacked off in these woods once.
But that was a long time ago when
everything rhymed a little with
the trees all facing upward and the sky
was full of itself and no one
was around. And everything smelled good.
I smelled good myself. A sweaty,
muddy, musky, burning smell of
autumn or late summer or very early
spring was in the air, and I was so
excited to be so young and existential
and solipsistic, that I peeled off my shirt
and pants and underpants and stood there,
erect and steeply rocking under a sycamore,
my peeled bark in a little pile at my feet,
my head tossing in the wind, my mouth
opening, wider, wider, as if trying
to pronounce all the vowels at the same time
and failing deliciously, and sinking down
to the ground, totally spent and spluttering
a few choice consonants like kisses meant
for the pursed lips of the wind.

My Visit to the Gardner Museum

Isabella Stewart Gardner had a lot of shit,
a lot of very old and beautiful shit
from all over the world, going all the way back
to the Egyptian sarcophagi, which look a lot like bathtubs
though really they're coffins. A whole lot of dead
shit in this museum, is what I'm thinking,
not sharing that thought with the lovely
woman who brought me here on our second date. To share
the world with the world, Isabella Stewart Gardner
built her eponymous museum in the Boston Fenway
in 1898. A hundred and ten years later,
me and Celia are walking through its galleries, not touching
because it's only our second date. And I think it's obscene
the way she accumulated all this shit and shipped it
back to Boston. And I think it's exactly what's wrong
with America, the way we keep appropriating
shit that doesn't belong to us, buying it up and
calling it ours. But I don't tell Celia that because I want
to hold her hand now, which is presently pointing up
at an enormous gilt frame with no painting in it,
her sweetly inquiring voice asking the well-ironed
museum guard standing next to it at attention: *What
is this?* And he tells us this is the Rembrandt
that was stolen a few years back, with the Vermeers
and other masterpieces cut right out
of their frames, the way poachers cut the valuable
part of the animal right out of the animal,
leaving the bloody carcass behind for the world
to stare at aghast and brokenhearted. And I think
this is by far the most interesting thing in the museum,
though I don't tell Celia that, her hand in mine now
as we listen together to the museum guard's harrowing tale
of the enemies of art breaking into Isabella's
rooms and ripping the Dutch masters right out. *Like a
rape,* she gasps, squeezing my hand tighter. That's when I
reach for her other hand, which she gives to me now,
so now we're standing face to face, just inches
away from each other's flesh-colored
flesh, which is making the museum guard very
uncomfortable. And he looks away. And I steal a kiss
from Celia. And then I cop a feel of Rubens.

Confessional Poem

People say they love my honesty, but honestly,
I'm a liar and a thief. I would steal your mother
and help you look for her. What was she wearing?
Large breasts or small? Truly, I have a prurient
bent. I sometimes incline towards pure prurience.
But at least I'm honest about it. I am up front
at the adult movie theater. I am in the first row
where there's nothing between me and these
fine actors, some of whom are really very fine—
I mean they're so convincing, I believe they are
in love. I believe I am in love. I mean that's how
good they are. But me, I'm not a good person. I would
pocket your twenty if I found it on the floor of
your car. I would borrow your car without asking you.
I would steal your line and put it in my poem without
crediting you. I would sleep with your mother
if she were good looking enough and willing. Honestly,
I am not an honest person and this poem is not
an honest poem. It expresses feelings and beliefs that
I have never felt or entertained. It's a sad day when
someone like you lets someone like me get away
with something like this. What were you thinking?

Bathroom Talk

A beautiful woman with a small dog, small breasts, foreign accent, stops me in the Public Garden and says: "Excuse me, do you know the bathroom?" And I wonder if the locative case in her native tongue is absorbed by the accusative case. And I wonder if the tongue is employed in a first kiss in a beach town of her native seashore, the waves lapping at our feet, as I look down in the general direction of her urinary tract and feet and say: "Yes. I know the bathroom very well." She smiles hopefully, gives me her great big brown expectant eyes, and says: "Yes?" And I feel a delicious pressure building in my chest, and in her chest, and in the air between us, a kind of referred pressure from her bladder or her colon, a kind of grammatical pressure from her tongue and my tongue which are meeting here in my favorite context. "Bathroom talk" my mother called it, banishing it from the house, and banishing us from the house when we couldn't stop laughing at the thought, couldn't stop crooning at the sound, and the sense, and the nonsense, and the signifiers and the signified. The nomenclature we invented as we went along, went about our business, which was the business of the body, the business of being in a body in the world, a world that preferred to keep that business secret, except for the children and the dogs and a few banished grown-ups. "Yes, yes," I tell her, and I hold out my hand to her, pointing with my other hand at the gold dome of the State House, where I'm headed myself, I tell her. It's the best-kept secret in the Commonwealth: the cleanest, most exquisite public toilets in the city flush and gleam there, flash and yearn there, there in that stately place, for patriots and foreigners alike. Though a dog, even a small dog, wouldn't be allowed in. No.

Dog Shit

I like to watch him sniff around for the perfect
place to void. I think this is the poetry of place
in his aesthetic universe, which is small but
surely very deeply felt. Look how discriminating
he is: *Here. No, here. No. On second thought,*
here. The same delicate choices you might make
in a poem. A poem about dog shit. He is brutally
honest as he turns and turns, shifts, lifts the inky
feather quill of his tail and quiveringly, yet firmly,
makes his mark, his nose in the wind, his eyes
tender, elsewhere, his mind on something I can't
read from here because it's already leaping ahead
to the next thought, the next scent, scene, figure,
landscape, the next new chapter, the next great poem.

Caveat

I should tell you that I sometimes get my latitudes
and longitudes mixed up. And also my apogees
and perigees. My stalactites and stalagmites sometimes
run together, not unlike my wants and my needs—
the wants drooling down, the needs piling up until
they form a kind of column, a shape like an hourglass
or a woman. My apologies in advance. I always forget
if bimonthly means twice a month or once every other,
and I can never remember the difference between
an iceberg and a glacier, or what 'desultory' means,
or even how to pronounce it. I have these gaps or
interstices. I have these spaces, these lapses and
incontinences. Plus my Arctic and my Antarctic
are hopelessly enmeshed. They're like totally mush.

Hardware Store

I love the names. Of the hardware. A kind of
software that isn't for sale because it's all
free. It feels like I'm browsing the stacks
of a library in another country in
my country, with titles I have never read
but heard of: rasps, levels, squares, planes,
ceiling hooks, corner braces, removable
pin hinges. I would like to read more
about removable pin hinges. I sidle up
and down aisle 3, looking seriously
for a thing for my door, a thing I don't
know the word for. They have strike plates
for push-button latches, and strike plates
for knob latches. And here are some door pivots
and swivel locks and keyed sash locks. A long-stem
heavy-duty roller. A pair of torsion spring cables.
I wonder what this universal T handle is for.
I would ask the hardware store guy but the thing is
I'm a guy myself, and I don't want him to know
I am hardware illiterate. So I continue my charade
of picking up each artifact, looking it over
thoughtfully, as though I knew the language,
as though I knew the landscape, as though
I weren't a stranger here myself.

Mediocrity Weeps to Behold Greatness

My new dentist
is admiring the great works
of my old dentist
in my mouth
and it makes me feel
like a museum of fine arts of sorts
with twenty years of gilded
masterpieces filling
my walls. He has never
seen such beautiful margins,
he says more to himself
than to me, incredulous
and impressed and more
than a little jealous
as he examines each one
with our mouths open,
tapping with his tiny round mirror
as if to wake us from
this dream of impossible beauty
and perfection. Thank you
doesn't seem the right
thing to say somehow, and yet
I say it anyway, with so many
amazed fingers camped out on my tongue
that it comes out sounding like
"hankie." That's when he abruptly
turns off the light
and wheels his stool away
somewhere behind me where I can't see him
wiping the tears from his eyes.

What It Looks Like

When my mother was dying
she said, "I'm not very good at this."
"Is anyone?" I asked, smoothing
the blanket on her hospital bed.
"Some people are," she said. "The ones
who spend their lives preparing."
"I think we're all unprepared," I said.
"I'm not very good at this," she said
again, wincing as she tried to change
position. "And what would it look like
if you were—good at this?" I asked
as I helped her rearrange the pillow.
She smiled at that, or at me, or maybe
at herself. And said, "I don't know."

Acknowledgments

The poems in *Bending the Notes* first appeared in the following magazines: *Bayou, Blueline, Carolina Quarterly, Coe Review, Comstock Review, Conte, Defenestration, FRiGG, Karamu, Off the Coast, Poetica, Poetry East, Shenandoah, Spoon River Poetry Review, Valparaiso Review, White Pelican Review*

The poems in *Dear Truth* first appeared in *Barefoot Muse, Big Toe Review, Bryant Literary Review, Comstock Review, Eclectica, Earth's Daughters, Faultline, Lalitamba, Oyez Review, The Pedestal, R.K.VR.Y., The Scrambler, Thick with Conviction, Tipton Poetry Journal, Upstreet.*

The poems in *A Little in Love a Lot* first appeared in *Alimentum, Bryant Literary Review, Coe Review, Diode, Eclectica, FutureCycle, Off the Coast, Poemeleon, Pure Francis, 2River Review, Sendero, Spillway, Toasted Cheese, Upstreet, Wild Goose Poetry Review.*

The poems in *Hurt Into Beauty* first appeared in *American Poetry Journal, Baltimore Review, Burnt District, Clerc Scar, Diode, Extracts, J Journal, Mount Hope, Pirene's Fountain, Right Hand Pointing, Solstice Literary Magazine, Terrain.org, Toasted Cheese, Wild Goose Poetry Review, Wordgathering.*

The poems in *Naming Names* first appeared in *A Narrow Fellow, Architrave, Best Poem, Blue Lyra Review, Bluestem, Bryant Literary Review, Chattahoochee Review, Coe Review, The 5-2 Crime Poetry Weekly, IthacaLit, Kill Author, Loch Raven Review, Off the Coast, Poemeleon, Poets & Artists, Red Booth Review, Rhino, Sleet, SubtleTea, Theodate, Toad, Upstreet, U.S. 1 Worksheets, Verdad.*

Cover artwork, "Colorful row of houses, N 35th and Meridian Ave N, Seattle, Washington, USA," by Wonderlane; author photo by Marlene Hostovsky; cover and interior book design by Diane Kistner (dkistner@futurecycle.org); Gentium Book Basic with Cronos Pro titling

About FutureCycle Press

FutureCycle Press is dedicated to publishing lasting English-language poetry books, chapbooks, and anthologies in both print-on-demand and ebook formats. Founded in 2007 by long-time independent editor/publishers and partners Diane Kistner and Robert S. King, the press incorporated as a nonprofit in 2012. A number of our editors are distinguished poets and writers in their own right, and we have been actively involved in the small press movement going back to the early seventies.

The FutureCycle Poetry Book Prize and honorarium is awarded annually for the best full-length volume of poetry we publish in a calendar year. Introduced in 2013, our Good Works projects are anthologies devoted to issues of universal significance, with all proceeds donated to a related worthy cause. Our Selected Poems series highlights contemporary poets with a substantial body of work to their credit; with this series we strive to resurrect work that has had limited distribution and is now out of print.

We are dedicated to giving all of the authors we publish the care their work deserves, making our catalog of titles the most diverse and distinguished it can be, and paying forward any earnings to fund more great books.

We've learned a few things about independent publishing over the years. We've also evolved a unique, resilient publishing model that allows us to focus mainly on vetting and preserving for posterity the most books of exceptional quality without becoming overwhelmed with bookkeeping and mailing, fundraising activities, or taxing editorial and production "bubbles." To find out more about what we are doing, come see us at www.futurecycle.org.